NOWHERE ELSE ON EARTH

Standing Tall for the Great Bear Rainforest

CAITLYN VERNON

SAVE THE RAINFOREST

ORCA BOOK PUBLISHERS

For my parents, Maggie and Phil,
for inspiring me and believing in me, always

Text copyright © 2011 Caitlyn Vernon

Library and Archives Canada Cataloguing in Publication

Vernon, Caitlyn, 1976-
Nowhere else on earth : standing tall for the Great
Bear Rainforest / by Caitlyn Vernon.

Issued also in electronic format.
ISBN 978-1-55469-303-0

1. Great Bear Rainforest (B.C.)--Juvenile literature.
2. Rain forest ecology--British Columbia--Juvenile literature.
3. Rain forest conservation--British Columbia--Juvenile
literature. 4. Environmental protection--Citizen participation--
Juvenile literature. 5. Temperate rain forests--British Columbia--
Juvenile literature. I. Title.
QH106.2.B7V47 2011   J577.34'097111   C2011-903458-1

First published in the United States, 2011
Library of Congress Control Number: 2011929247

Summary: A hands-on guide to the magic and majesty of British Columbia's Great Bear Rainforest,
with suggestions for activism in any community.

*Orca Book Publishers is dedicated to preserving the environment and has printed this book on paper certified
by the Forest Stewardship Council®. The interior paper is 100% recycled (100% PCW) and printed with vegetable-based inks.*

Orca Book Publishers gratefully acknowledges the support for its publishing programs provided by the
following agencies: the Government of Canada through the Canada Book Fund and the Canada Council for the Arts,
and the Province of British Columbia through the BC Arts Council and the Book Publishing Tax Credit.

Cover design by Teresa Bubela
Interior design by Nadja Penaluna
Illustrations by Mike Deas
Maps by Dave Leversee
Author photo by Frances Litman
Cover photos: main image by TJ Watt; side images (from top) by Mike Ambach, Douglas Neasloss, Miles Ritter,
Andrew S. Wright, Ian McAllister, Caitlyn Vernon, Marven Robinson. Back cover photo by Andrew S. Wright.

ORCA BOOK PUBLISHERS
PO Box 5626, Stn. B
Victoria, BC Canada
V8R 6S4

ORCA BOOK PUBLISHERS
PO Box 468
Custer, WA USA
98240-0468

www.orcabook.com
Printed and bound in Canada.

14 13 12 11 • 4 3 2 1

OPPOSITE: A grizzly bear and
a bald eagle share the shoreline
in the Great Bear Rainforest.
ANDREW S. WRIGHT

CONTENTS

INTRODUCTION

Bear Witness

A black bear walks into a Subway restaurant in the small town of Kitimat, in northern British Columbia. Sounds like the first line of a joke, doesn't it? But it's no joke when the bear jumps over the counter and pokes its nose into the sandwich fixings. You can watch the video online. The young woman working that day hid in the bathroom while the bear sniffed around. After the bear left the Subway, it was shot because people were worried it would come back into town. That's what happens when bears eat sandwiches instead of salmon.

This black bear lived in the Great Bear Rainforest, on the north coast of British Columbia. The rainforest is a magical place, where edible plants, fish from the ocean and tiny creatures in the soil are all connected. People live among the giant trees too, and whales swim offshore. Wolf pups play with ravens on the beach, and eagles soar overhead, teaching their young to catch fish. Spirit bears roam the forest, their white fur standing out against the many shades of green. Moss grows thick on tree branches,

"I can't stand it when people say, 'I'm just one person; I can't make a difference.' If everybody says that, nothing ever gets done. You have to say, 'I'm one person; maybe I can get others to join me.'"

—Caitlin Chestnut (14), peace activist (from *It's Our World, Too!* by Phillip Hoose)

OPPOSITE: A curious coastal wolf pup plays with kelp.
MARVEN ROBINSON

TAKE ACTION

We can change the ending

Since each of us is a character in both our own story and the shared story of the Earth, what happens next depends on what we choose to do. If we don't like the way the story is unfolding, we can change it. It's often not easy, because other characters in the story may resist change, but depending on the actions we take and the choices we make in our own lives, we can help give the story a different ending.

Kids in Bella Bella speak up for wild salmon.
CRISTINA MITTERMEIER / iLCP

"Every great dream begins with a dreamer. Always remember, you have within you the strength, the patience, and the passion to reach for the stars to change the world."
—Harriet Tubman, African-American abolitionist (1820–1913)

A bald eagle. JENS WIETING

where seabirds have their nests. Slugs and bugs build the rich soil that ancient trees depend on.

Salmon travel up the rivers and streams from the ocean into the rainforest. In a good year, grizzly bears will eat so many salmon that their bellies actually drag on the ground. When the bears want to nap after eating so much, they dig pits in the ground to rest their big bellies in. Sounds like a good life, doesn't it?

But things are changing in the Great Bear Rainforest. Bears on the coast depend on salmon—not Subway sandwiches—to fatten up before their winter **hibernation** *(words in bold can be found in the Glossary on page 122)*. In recent years the bears have often been hungry. In one community, six bears were shot in a single week for wandering into town. When fewer salmon return up the rivers, the bears come into town to eat apples in the orchards.

Up and down the coast, people tell stories about salmon. Stories about how many there used to be, and how few

there are these days. Stories about how skinny the bears are because they don't have enough salmon to eat. You hear about streams where only three hundred salmon returned instead of the usual three thousand. You hear that when someone brought fish from elsewhere and threw them on the banks of one of these streams, the bears ran like hungry dogs to get the salmon. What is going on in the rainforest?

Why Get Involved?

Learning about the state of our Earth can be upsetting. How is it that there are so few wild salmon and the bears are starving? Why is this happening? And what can we do about it?

It's normal to get upset about some of the things that you see in your world, such as war, oil spills, animals becoming

Spirit bears, also known as Kermode bears, are a rare type of black bear. DOUGLAS NEASLOSS

ECO-STORY

Surprising a bear

The summer I turned eight, I backpacked part of the West Coast Trail on Vancouver Island with my parents. One day I followed a bird into the tall grasses beside the beach where we were camping. All of a sudden I came face to face with a young black bear! The best thing to do when you see a black bear is to talk to it quietly, let it know you mean no harm and slowly back away. But I did exactly what you're not supposed to do: I turned and ran back to my parents. Fortunately, the bear was equally surprised. Just as I got back to my parents, the bear went bounding past us down the beach.

Since then, I have been fortunate to see many bears. Bears eating blueberries, bears on high mountain ridges in the moonlight, bears fishing for salmon. Each time I see a bear, I feel lucky. I thank the bear for sharing its home with me, and I give it lots of space.

A black bear marks a tree with its scent
ANDREW S. WRIGHT

DID YOU KNOW

Are the bears the real problem?

Bears that become comfortable around humans and learn to associate us with food are called "problem bears." Like the bear that walked into the Subway, they are often shot. But is it really the bears that are the problem? Bears approach humans for several reasons: we have destroyed their natural **habitat** and they have nowhere else to live; we have fished all the salmon and they are hungry; we leave our garbage lying around and they think it smells good. From this perspective, it is humans that are causing the problems.

A youth activist calls on world leaders to take action on climate change.
GREENPEACE / CHRISTIAN ÅSLUND

extinct or the inequalities between rich and poor. You might feel sad or angry or discouraged. Sometimes it seems easiest to deal with these feelings by turning away and pretending the problems don't exist. But you might want to do something to help make things better.

Even when you want to do something, the problems can seem so huge that you don't know where to start. The good news is that doing one small thing can make a big difference. In this book you're going to read about people who are helping the bears and the salmon in the rainforest. When you look around and see so many other concerned people who are speaking up for the rainforest and taking action for a more **sustainable** future, it can be inspiring. It's been said many times before, but it's worth saying again: Together we can make a difference.

I hope the stories in this book will help you find ways of getting involved in the world that feel right to you. It doesn't matter how old you are. Young people have voices too, and there is power in speaking out about things that bother or hurt you. Also, taking action can often make you feel better about yourself and about the world. You can never determine the outcome of your actions; all you can do is take one step at a time in the right direction.

Making Choices

The bear that ambled into the Subway came to tell us something. We need to take the time to listen: for the fish, for the bears, for all the people who live on the coast and for those of us who care about the Earth. This book

Strength in numbers

I remember sitting in the backseat, looking out the window as my parents drove across Vancouver Island. There was a stretch of highway where the mountains on both sides looked like they had been shaved. Large **clear-cuts** had taken all the trees off entire mountains, from top to bottom. One year we made our way through these clear-cuts to visit Meares Island, a small island where the trees were still standing and a struggle was brewing to save the ancient forests. I was eight years old at the time, and the trees seemed huge! Seeing these big trees helped me understand what had been lost when the forests along the highway had been logged, and I wondered what happened to all the wildlife that had lived there. How would the bears and the eagles and the frogs survive?

In this way, I grew up knowing that there was a lot to worry about in the world. But I also grew up knowing that it was possible to do something about the things that concern you. On Meares Island, the Tla-o-qui-aht and the Ahousaht **First Nations**, with the support of environmental groups, set up a blockade and prevented the forest company from logging the island. The big trees that I saw that year are still there, still standing.

As a kid I spent time on picket lines and in marches and demonstrations. I listened to my dad sing songs at rallies, inspiring workers to demand fair wages and safe working conditions. I was surrounded by my mom's friends, who witnessed the violence toward women in the world and fought to stop it. I grew up knowing that it was thanks to generations of activists that women got the right to vote, that child labor was made illegal in North America and that workers got a weekend. At an early age I learned the powerful feeling of marching with thousands of other people who share your concerns and your vision for how the world could be. I learned that you don't win them all, but there is strength in numbers and often you *can* make a difference.

TJ WATT

is about listening to the voices from the coast and noticing what is happening around us. It is about bearing witness to loss. And it is about taking action. Understanding and acknowledging the difficulties we are facing puts us in a good position to do something about it.

CHAPTER ONE

The Great Bear Rainforest

Where Is the Great Bear Rainforest?

The Great Bear Rainforest is a Canadian **coastal temperate rainforest** located on the central and north coast of British Columbia (BC). It stretches from just above Bute Inlet all the way up the coast to the bottom of the Alaskan Panhandle. The Great Bear Rainforest covers an area about the size of Switzerland.

A Coastal Temperate Rainforest

There are many different kinds of forest on this planet. On the east coast of North America there are **deciduous forests** that turn beautiful shades of red and orange before they lose their leaves in the fall. In the north there is the **boreal forest**, where the **climate** is so harsh that trees grow really slowly and stay quite small. On the west coast of North America there is a thin strip of forest that stays

MAP: Between the mountains and the ocean lies BC's Great Bear Rainforest.

OPPOSITE: Coastal temperate rainforest at Rose Harbour, Haida Gwaii. ANDREW S. WRIGHT

green all year round and is called the coastal temperate rainforest. Globally, this is an extremely rare type of forest. Even before any industrial logging took place, coastal temperate rainforests covered less than 0.2 percent of the Earth's land surface.

Coastal temperate rainforests are only found along the west coasts of continents. Countries with this kind of forest include Canada, the United States, Chile, New Zealand, Australia, Norway, Taiwan and Japan. Many of these forests around the world have been logged. The Great Bear Rainforest contains the largest unlogged coastal temperate rainforest in the world.

Big Ancient Trees

BC's coastal temperate rainforest is home to some of the oldest and largest trees on Earth. Two of the top five tallest types of trees in the world grow here: the coastal Douglas-fir and the Sitka spruce. On the west coast of North America, western red cedars and yellow cedars can live up to about

TOP: A black bear cub climbs a spruce tree. JENS WIETING

BOTTOM: Devil's club has sharp spines and can be used as medicine. CAITLYN VERNON

RIGHT: In the Great Bear Rainforest, some black bears have spirit bear cubs. DOUGLAS NEASLOSS

2,000 years. One yellow cedar in southern coastal BC is known to be 1,835 years old. The trunks of western red cedar trees can be as wide as 6 meters (20 feet) in diameter. Just outside Vancouver, a 126-meter (415-foot) Douglas-fir was chopped down in 1902. That tree was 38 stories high!

Plenty of Plants

Massive trees covered in thick green moss aren't the only plants in the rainforest. There are also tasty berries, edible plants and plants that can be used for medicine. There are plants that sting you, plants that poke you with their sharp spines, and others with leaves so soft you can use them as toilet paper. There are plants that existed during the time of the dinosaurs. There are plants so small and delicate you have to look hard to notice them, and others with leaves so big they block the sun and the rain.

Amazing Animals and Beautiful Birds

Animals of all sizes live in the rainforest. There are wolves, deer, mountain goats, elk, bats, northern flying squirrels and the elusive marten. Eagles build their nests on trees overlooking the oceans, and ravens play on the wind. All kinds of insects live in the forest, including **species** of beetles found nowhere else in the world. Woodpeckers live off the insects in dead or decaying trees, leaving holes behind that are then used by owls and other birds for their nests. And of course, there are the bears. The rare white spirit bear, also known as Kermode bear, is a genetic variation of the black bear and is found nowhere else on Earth.

DID YOU KNOW

Shake hands with a tree

You can identify a tree by its bark, needles, cones and the shape of the tree itself. For example, if you "shake hands" with a young spruce, by grabbing a branch, the needles feel sharp and prickly. In comparison, the branches of a western hemlock feel soft to the touch. But western hemlocks can be most easily identified by looking at their tops, which droop over as if a bird has just been sitting on it. A red cedar is known by its stringy bark and flat needles. And Douglas-fir cones are easy to identify. Under each scale it looks as if a mouse ran in to hide, with just its back legs and tail sticking out. Wherever you live, the trees will have characteristics that you can learn in order to tell them apart.

Western screech owls nest in tree cavities. JARED HOBBS

Marbled murrelets, nicknamed *mamu* by scientists, are small seabirds that spend most of their lives on the ocean but nest in the branches of old-growth trees. Instead of building a nest, the marbled murrelets simply lay one egg in a mossy mat on a tree branch. The branch has to be wide enough that the egg, and then the chick once it hatches, doesn't fall off. For this reason marbled murrelets can only nest in old-growth trees, where the branches are at least 15 to 75 centimeters (6 to 30 inches) across. When the chick is ready to leave the nest, it jumps off the branch and has to learn how to fly on its first try. And if that isn't amazing enough, the young bird then flies all the way back to the ocean by itself and somehow knows how to find food once it gets there.

As more and more old-growth trees are logged, there are fewer good nesting sites available. Marbled murrelets are now at risk of becoming an **endangered species**.

Spectacular Sea Life

Orcas, humpback whales, porpoises, seals and sea lions live in the ocean off the coast of the rainforest. Along the beaches and rocky shorelines you will discover many edible creatures, such as clams, scallops, mussels and oysters. Kelp beds are home to crabs, sea otters and numerous fish, such as kelp greenling and kelp perch. Salmon swim upriver from the ocean into the forest.

A Place for People

The Great Bear Rainforest is also home to many people. Archaeology tells us that First Nations have lived here for over nine thousand years. First Nations people say they

TOP: Bringing in the halibut catch of the day. THOMAS P. PESCHAK

BOTTOM: A landscape carved by glaciers. ANDREW S. WRIGHT

have always been here, since time before memory. With **colonization**, settlers arrived from Europe and Asia to live and work on the coast. In the Great Bear Rainforest there are a few small towns and only one city, Prince Rupert. Many of the people who live in the Great Bear Rainforest today are First Nations.

Getting There

Imagine you are taking a trip into the Great Bear Rainforest. From Vancouver, you can drive or fly to Prince Rupert on the north coast or to the little town of Bella Coola on the central coast. You can also fly directly to

"Every morning I awake torn between a desire to save the world and an inclination to savor it. This makes it hard to plan the day. But if we forget to savor the world, what possible reason do we have for saving it? In a way, the savoring must come first."

—**E.B. White**, American author (1899–1985)

ECO-STORY

Snakes in my shirt

When I was a kid, I spent a lot of time exploring the outdoors, even though I grew up mostly in a city. I went hiking and kayaking, climbed trees, caught snakes and frogs, and explored the wonders of **tide pools**. I studied biology in university so that I could get work that took me outside. I've researched beetles that live in trees, counted fish in streams and done plant surveys. In one job I flew in a helicopter every day to study wildlife habitat in remote valleys.

Over time I have come to realize that it's not the wildlife that we need to manage; it's ourselves. We use wood products, we eat meat and salmon, and we mine minerals from the earth to make computers, cell phones, windmills, jewelry, fuel and so much more. I now understand how important it is to take only what we need so that **ecosystems** stay healthy. Not just for the sake of the plants and animals, but also because we depend on these ecosystems for almost everything in our lives.

The author as a young girl, going hiking. PHIL VERNON

Dancing a raven mask,
on Haida Gwaii.
MIKE AMBACH

Bella Bella, west of Bella Coola. From any of these places you will need to take a boat, floatplane, kayak or canoe to get to the other communities. Whichever way you travel, what you see will be amazing.

If you are flying from Vancouver, you will be going north and the ocean will be on the left-hand side of the airplane. You will see islands covered in scrubby forest and brownish bogs. On your right is the coastal mountain range, a long line of snowcapped peaks and glaciers. Between the open ocean and the mountains is the coastal temperate rainforest. **Fjords**—long narrow fingers of ocean—cut inland. Trees cling to the steep sides of granite hills. Looking down from the plane, you will see the dark green of ancient trees in river valleys. In some of the valleys there are large patches where clear-cut logging has removed all the trees. If the logging is recent, the clear-cuts look brown; if the logging was some time ago, young trees are growing back and the area is light green.

To get to the remote coastal communities you might choose to take a floatplane. These planes can only fly if there

VOICES FROM THE COAST

In search of seagull eggs

Jantina Azak (15), Gitga'at First Nation

"One time I went seagull egg gathering and found a couple of seagull eggs. I like living on the coast because I'm able to go whale watching, and bear viewing. We go clam and cockle digging, kayaking. And it is not big like a city. All of this is a big change for me because I just moved here to Hartley Bay a couple of years ago. I used to live in Gitwinksihlkw [formerly known as Canyon City, in northern BC] and I never got to do any of these activities. I know that if something bad were to happen and these foods got contaminated, I wouldn't be able to have these foods or do these things anymore."

is clear visibility. Your flight might be delayed because it is often foggy on the coast. But the wait is worth it. Flying in a floatplane is exciting, especially if you are lucky enough to get the seat up front next to the pilot. The floatplanes that fly around the Great Bear Rainforest have names like the Beaver, the Otter and the Goose. The Goose is a pretty wild ride; instead of landing on pontoons like other floatplanes, it actually lands on its belly in the water. As you land, the waves come crashing up right outside your window!

You can also take a boat to get into the Great Bear Rainforest. This is a good way to really see what is happening on the water and get a closer view of the coastline. As you travel up the coast, perhaps in a sailboat or a fishing boat, you might see big barges transporting logs. If you are lucky, there will be whales in the distance, porpoises will come and play in the boat's wake or you might see a raft of sea otters resting in some kelp. As you pass the **estuaries** (where rivers

A Place for People

Lax Kw'alaams
Metlakatla • Prince • Terrace
Old Massett • Rupert • Kitimat
Queen Charlotte City • Kitkatla • Kitamaat Village
Skidegate • Hartley Bay
Sandspit • Klemtu •
Bella Bella •
• Bella Coola
• Wuikinuxv Village (Rivers Inlet)
• Kingcome
Port Hardy •
Alert Bay

Cities and towns in and around the Great Bear Rainforest are home to many people.

meet the sea), look closely—there may be bears digging for edible roots. From a sailboat, because it is quiet, you might hear the howling of wolves. You will pass dilapidated old buildings and wharves that are falling into the water, the ruins of what once were thriving canneries.

For an even closer look at what is happening around you, you'll have to get into a canoe or a kayak. From a small boat like this, you might be lucky enough to catch a glimpse of a wolf on the beach or a deer swimming between islands. Sea stars and anemones line the rocky shorelines, and sea lions are often hauled out on rocks. A curious seal might swim up to you. Chances are, the rainforest will live up to its name and you will get rained on.

When you arrive in a First Nations community like Klemtu or Hartley Bay, you will see boats moored at a dock and houses facing the water. In some cases there is a **big house**, a large wooden building used for cultural events and community gatherings. Almost all the communities have roads and cars, even though the roads don't go very far beyond the town, and cars can only get there by barge or ferry. The exception is Hartley Bay, which has board-walks instead of roads. Even though the entire town is only the size of a couple of city blocks, people zoom around on rainproof golf carts.

I Don't Live There, So Why Does the Great Bear Rainforest Matter to Me?

The health of the Great Bear Rainforest matters a great deal to all of us, wherever we live. As a large and mostly intact forest, it plays many important ecological roles: it releases oxygen we all breathe; it absorbs carbon dioxide, which helps to slow **climate change**; it regulates global **water cycles**; and it maintains **biodiversity**.

The Great Bear Rainforest is a source of salmon and other seafood, as well as paper and wood products. Plants from the rainforest are used in hair products and cosmetics and medicines. It is also a place to see bears and whales in the wild, and to reconnect to a world that includes ancient trees.

"You are not Atlas carrying the world on your shoulder. It is good to remember that the planet is carrying you."
—Vandana Shiva,
Indian physicist, author and environmental activist (1952–)

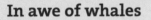

ECO-STORY

In awe of whales

Even from far away, the sound of a whale breathing travels clearly across the water. As a whale surfaces, it releases air from its blowhole with a loud *phooof* and a plume of spray. If it is an orca, or killer whale, the next thing you see is a black dorsal fin rising out of the water and then slowly sinking back down. If it is a humpback whale, you'll see its back sliding over and under the water, and then its tail will gracefully emerge as the whale dives down deep.

One day I was on a boat that had a **hydrophone**, a microphone that works underwater. We turned off the boat engine and drifted while a pod, or family, of killer whales swam past. Over the hydrophone I could hear the cry of the baby whale and the clicks of **echolocation**, the sounds that killer whales make in order to navigate underwater and find food. To me, the echolocation sounded like a Ping Pong ball being bounced on a table.

Another day I saw something that looked like a log floating in the water. Except that every once in a while it would lift up a little, let out a plume of spray and then sink back down. This "log" was actually a sleeping humpback whale!

There is something about a whale that demands respect. It doesn't seem to matter where I am or who I'm with—when a whale surfaces, everyone holds their breath and goes silent for a moment to watch.

Humpback whales.
ANDREW S. WRIGHT

CHAPTER TWO

Salmon in the Trees, Wolves on the Beach

The Great Bear Rainforest exists in the space between ocean and mountains, the place where land and water come together. The boundary is blurred, with marine life coming into the forest and forest animals swimming in the ocean. There are **nutrients** from salmon in the trees...but how do they get there?

Where Land and Sea Meet: Adapting in the intertidal zone

The **intertidal zone** is the part of the shoreline that is covered by water at high tide and exposed at low tide. For the creatures that live here, this is a harsh environment. To survive, an animal or plant has to be comfortable spending hours underwater as well as hours exposed to the sun. Most plants and animals have adapted to one

"There are two ways to live your life. One is as though nothing is a miracle. And the other is as though everything is."
—Albert Einstein, physicist (1879–1955)

OPPOSITE: Salmon make a good meal for a coastal wolf.
IAN MCALLISTER

environment or the other. Fish spend their entire lives underwater and have developed a way to get oxygen out of the water without having to come up for air. Desert plants can survive extended droughts with no water. But to be able to live underwater *and* to live exposed to drought and sunlight, and to constantly be switching back and forth between the two worlds, is quite a feat!

Many of the animals in the intertidal zone are colorful and creative. You never know what you might find when you poke around in tide pools. Barnacles are stuck to rocks by their heads and eat with their purple feathery feet. When barnacles are underwater, their shells open up and you can see their feet waving about. Sea stars, commonly called starfish, are purple or red or orange. They are fierce **predators** that eat by sticking their stomachs out from their bodies over oyster or mussel shells, prying them open and sucking

TOP: Blood star, a kind of sea star.
JENS WIETING

BOTTOM: A great blue heron rests on a floating mat of kelp.
JARED HOBBS

RIGHT: An estuary is where a river meets the ocean.
DANIEL BELTRA

the creatures out. If you are very patient, you might see a sea star moving around and hunting for food. Hermit crabs scuttle around in tide pools, wearing borrowed snail shells. Sea anemones look like flowers when underwater and then close up and cover themselves with bits of shell to keep cool and moist when the tide goes out. Clams and scallops live under sandy beaches, moving around by squirting water out between their shells.

Why Does It Rain So Much in the Rainforest?

Did you know that all the fresh water in the world (except for the water stored as ice in glaciers)—the water we drink, shower in and use to flush our toilets and water our gardens—is constantly in motion? When it rains on land, the water flows down the tree trunks into the soil, into lakes and rivers and eventually down into the ocean. Of course, the water in the ocean is too salty to drink. But fortunately for us, water **evaporates** off the surface of the ocean and forms clouds. Some of these clouds are blown toward land by wind and storms. When clouds reach the coastal mountains, they drop their moisture in the form of rain or snow. This is where our fresh water comes from: rain, snow and the melting of glaciers high up in the mountains. It is these clouds coming off the ocean that make the coastal temperate rainforest so very wet. It rains and rains, and everything stays lush and green.

DID YOU KNOW

Wolves prefer salmon brains

Wolves are fussy eaters. They eat only the head and leave the rest of the salmon behind. Why so fussy? Apparently there is a parasite that lives in the guts of salmon that can kill a wolf. Through years of **evolution**, wolves have learned that it isn't safe to eat more than the brain of a salmon.

As a result, when a wolf pack is done eating and moves on, it leaves behind hundreds of headless salmon scattered along the riverbank. This helps ensure that the wolves can keep eating salmon for years to come. How does this work? The remains of the salmon add valuable nutrients to the forest floor and the streams. They provide food for plants and insects, which then provide the necessary habitat and food for the salmon when they emerge from their eggs. The young salmon then head out to sea, and when they return to spawn, the wolves once again have something to eat.

Wolves fishing for salmon.
MARVEN ROBINSON

Being beside the ocean also influences the temperature of the rainforest. In winter, when the middle of North America is covered in snow, the ocean keeps the coast of BC mild and wet and green. And in summer, when places far inland are really hot and dry, the ocean keeps the coastal forests cool and moist. It is this mild and rainy climate that allows the trees to grow so big.

VOICES FROM THE COAST

Why is that man sitting in the river?

Dr. Tom Reimchen

Dr. Tom Reimchen is a biologist at the University of Victoria. His research takes him to the central and north coast of BC, to the rivers and streams where bears feed on the spawning salmon. Why would he choose to spend his days, and sometimes even his nights, surrounded by rotting salmon and hungry bears? He says it can be stressful, scary, exciting and unpredictable.

Tom is trying to find out just how connected the ocean and the forest really are. Because of Tom and other scientists, we know that nutrients from salmon are feeding the forest. By watching the bears as they eat the salmon, biologists have estimated that up to 80 percent of the salmon that enter streams end up on the forest floor. On one stream, each bear hauled about five hundred salmon into the forest!

Tom's research is important because it illustrates how nothing is wasted in nature. There is no leftover salmon. The parts of the salmon not eaten by bears feed the streams, the insects, the birds, the trees and other wildlife. Tom sets traps to catch insects, takes samples of wood from trees and cuts tiny pieces off the feathers of birds caught in nets and then studies these samples in a laboratory. In this way, he has found evidence of marine nutrients in insects, treetops and even in the feathers of birds. Tom's research also gives us a way to find out if there used to be salmon in a stream where now there are none. If the trees along the stream contain evidence of marine nutrients, we know that salmon used to spawn there.

Does the Ocean Need the Forest?

When you think of the ocean, do you think of the forest too? Probably not. We generally think of the ocean and the forest as two separate things. But it's not so simple. There are lots of connections between the ocean and the forest.

It's not just by chance that many marine animals spend so much time along the edge of the forest. The water that flows down through the forest soil and eventually into the ocean brings a steady stream of nutrients and minerals that are food for ocean creatures. Both small and large sea life inhabit this area. Gray whales often feed near the shoreline, where they dive down to the ocean floor and suck up mouthfuls of sand and mud and tiny animals. They squirt out the water and mud and eat the tiny animals and worms left behind. Crabs live in kelp beds and estuaries where rivers meet the ocean.

Salmon spend most of their lives in the ocean, but they also need forests. They are born in rivers, where the young salmon depend on the forest to provide food, shelter and shade from the sun.

Does the Forest Need the Ocean?

Forests near the ocean get lots of rain and have a mild climate, good for growing big rainforest trees. But one of the most amazing ways the forest depends on the ocean is this: there are salmon in the trees. Well, not exactly. They don't swim there, but nutrients from the ocean have been found at the tops of trees.

How does this work? Bears, otters, wolves and eagles drag salmon out of the rivers to be eaten in the safety of the forest. The parts of the salmon they don't eat **decompose**

BOTTOM: Halibut live on the ocean floor. When salmon are spawning, the halibut come nearer to shore to eat the bits of dead salmon that wash out of the rivers and into the ocean.

CRISTINA MITTERMEIER / iLCP

and eventually turn into soil. It's like when you put fertilizer on your garden to help make your plants grow. The marine nutrients that were in the salmon end up in the soil, where they can be absorbed by tree roots.

VOICES FROM THE COAST

A picture is worth a thousand words
Ian McAllister, activist and photographer

Ian lives with his wife and two children near the small community of Shearwater in the Great Bear Rainforest. He says that his work to protect the Great Bear Rainforest is exciting, challenging and fulfilling. It's also very diverse. Through his foundation, Pacific Wild, Ian directs research and film projects and educates people about the rainforest. He has to be able to captain a boat, scuba dive, climb trees, catch salmon and live in remote locations for extended periods of time. Ian finds inspiration in the very place that he is working to protect. He is motivated by knowing that we can save wildlife habitat that would be destroyed if we sat back and did nothing.

Ian says he started taking photographs because it was difficult to find words to describe how special the Great Bear Rainforest is. Plus, he enjoys the creative challenge of photographing wildlife like bears and wolves, and of trying to capture a special moment with his camera.

Ian's children accept that they share their home (but not their house!) with grizzly bears and packs of wolves. Ian is worried that the experiences he and his family enjoy may not be possible for future generations. He says that changes are happening so fast they are almost impossible for humans to gauge and monitor. He sees salmon slowly disappearing from the creeks and rivers of the rainforest, and as they decline, so will many other species that rely on them. But he is hopeful because, unlike other ecosystems on the planet that are already gone and need to be restored, the Great Bear Rainforest still supports so much life, human culture and diversity. "We simply have to protect what we already have," he says. "Nothing could be simpler really." Ian's beautiful photos do a lot to help raise awareness about the rainforest and the need to protect it.

PHOTO OF IAN MCALLISTER BY PAUL NICKLEN

IAN MCALLISTER

In other words, the salmon provide food for the trees! Trees actually grow faster in years when there is a good salmon run because of all the rich nutrients that are made available for the soil.

Life Cycle of a Salmon

Pacific salmon are born in fresh water, spend their adult lives in the salty ocean, and then return to the rivers and lakes where they were born to spawn and to die.

Adult salmon travel thousands of kilometers all over the North Pacific Ocean in schools or groups of fish, eating smaller fish, shrimp and plankton (microscopic plants and animals). After two to seven years of living in the ocean, when it's time to lay their eggs, adult salmon return to the exact stream they were born in. How they find their way back remains a mystery. Scientists think that the salmon use a combination of **celestial navigation** (the stars) and an internal **magnetic compass** to find their way around the ocean and back to the coast. Once they reach the coast, they use their sense of smell to find their river. They are able to find their way back to the stream where they were born on the first try, without being shown the way or taught how to do this. And, amazingly, they all arrive at the same time. During the long journey from the ocean to their spawning stream—some travel as far as 3,300 kilometers (2,000 miles) up rivers—the salmon don't eat anything at all.

If you are lucky enough to live near a river where salmon spawn, you can watch them battle their way upstream. When they finally arrive home, the females

DID YOU KNOW

How the cedar trees came north

Cedar trees haven't always grown along the coast of BC. Ten thousand years ago most of the coast was covered in glaciers. Nothing grew here then. As the glaciers retreated, plants and animals moved north into this area. The animals just walked. But how did the plants and trees move north?

A cedar tree produces cones. Each cone contains many seeds, and each tiny seed has the capability to grow into a large tree. Cedar trees that had survived south of the glaciers moved north as their seeds were blown north by the wind. As the temperatures warmed up and soil formed after the glaciers retreated, cedar seeds started to land in places suitable for growing. Eventually, the conditions were right along the coast of BC for these seeds to grow into ancient trees.

Pink salmon wait under a small waterfall before continuing upstream to their spawning grounds.
THOMAS P. PESCHAK

A coastal wolf pauses in the intertidal zone to check out the photographer.
IAN MCALLISTER

deposit eggs in hollows dug into the gravel, and the males fertilize the eggs. This is called spawning. After spawning, the adult salmon die. The decaying salmon are eaten by birds, wildlife and insects.

When salmon first hatch from the eggs, they live off the yolk sac attached to their body. They remain under the gravel for protection from predators until they have absorbed all the nutrients from their yolk sac and need to find other food. After up to four months, they swim up from the gravel to start feeding on tiny insects and plants.

There are five types of Pacific salmon—Chinook, coho, chum, sockeye and pink—and each lives in fresh water for a different length of time before heading to the ocean. On their way out to sea the salmon pass through the estuary, where there is a mix of fresh and salt water. Once in the ocean, the salmon grow into adults. And the cycle continues.

Coastal Wolves

The wolves of the Great Bear Rainforest inhabit the area between land and sea. They even spend some of their time in the sea and have been known to swim as far as 10 kilometers (6.2 miles) through open ocean to reach

VOICES FROM THE COAST

Food from all around
Rachel Lynne-Dell Hill (16), Gitga'at First Nation

"My favorite food that comes from the ocean is octopus because it tastes really good. My favorite food that comes from the beach is probably cockles. And my favorite food that comes out of the rainforest is deer."

an island! On land these wolves will eat deer, moose, mountain goats and even the occasional black bear. But much of their diet comes from the sea, and they eat just about everything, including salmon, crabs, clams and barnacles. They swim out to small islands and kill seals that have hauled themselves out on the rocks. And if a sea lion, squid or whale gets beached on the shore, the wolves will eat that too.

Even though much of their food comes from the ocean, coastal wolves also depend on the **old-growth forests**. The big trees are really important for raising wolf pups in the summer. Wolves take care of their pups in tunnels and dens dug under the bases of large old trees. And throughout the winter when there are no salmon in the rivers, the wolves hunt deer in the old-growth forests.

One way to find the wolves is to look for ravens. Ravens seem to like to be near wolves. After wolves have made a kill, ravens will fly down and eat beside them. The young wolf pups play on the beach with the ravens. The pups chase the ravens; the ravens dive down and pull at the pups' ears!

Bears Eat Barnacles

The place where a river meets the ocean is called an estuary. In an estuary there are few clear boundaries between land and sea. Where river valleys become wide and flat as they meet the sea, the water that has been rushing down mountainsides spreads out and moves more slowly. As it slows, silt and sand settle out of the water and build up into islands in the middle of the river.

Grizzly bear munching on sedges in an estuary.
DOUGLAS NEASLOSS

TAKE ACTION

Animal tracks

What animals live near you? If they keep themselves well hidden, you can know if they have been around by looking for the tracks they leave behind. A good place to find tracks is in mud, wet sand or snow, where you can clearly see the imprints from their feet. Each animal has a distinctive track that you can learn to identify. Can you tell the difference between the tracks of a wolf and a dog? (Hint: one is much bigger.) Did you know that the front feet of bears leave footprints that are different from their back feet? Tracks can tell us not just what animals live in the area, but also how long ago the animal passed by, what direction it was going and even if it was walking, running or being chased. Once we learn how to read the signs, tracks give us a window into the lives of animals.

Black bear tracks on a beach.
DOUGLAS NEASLOSS

The water twists and turns around these small islands where tall green grasses grow. From the air, an estuary looks like a bunch of puzzle pieces that have been separated by meandering water.

In spring, when hungry bears emerge from hibernation, the salmon are not yet coming up the rivers. At this time, bears depend on the plants in the estuaries for food. Bears are **omnivores**, which means they eat both meat and plants. One of the bears' favorite foods is Lyngby's sedge, a tall grasslike plant that grows in estuaries. They also like the roots of the rice root lily, also known as the chocolate lily. It's easy to tell where a bear has been eating in an estuary because the ground is all dug up and full of holes.

On the beaches and along the intertidal zone, grizzly bears eat clams, crabs and mussels—seafood that is also eaten by First Nations people on the coast. Bears even eat barnacles! And like the wolves, grizzly bears go into the forest to make their dens. Bear dens, used for their winter hibernation, are usually found below large old-growth trees, high up on the sides of mountains.

Bears, wolves and people inhabit the area between land and sea. All are connected to the salmon, which make the journey from the forest to the ocean and then back to the forest, in an endless cycle of life.

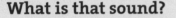

ECO-STORY

What is that sound?

Walking along the edge of the ocean is one of my favorite things to do. Sometimes I put on my gumboots and wade right into the water, or run as fast as I can along the beach, weaving in and out with the waves. Other times I like to stand with my eyes closed and listen. To me, it always sounds like the ocean is breathing as the waves rush in and then get sucked back out, again and again, never stopping, always there. There is something about the sound that quiets my mind.

Sometimes I like to poke around in tide pools and look for crabs under rocks. To get to know a place well, you've got to get it under your nails. Touch things, smell them, get your hands dirty. The red and purple sea stars that hug the undersides of rocks feel surprisingly bumpy and tough. When I reach into tide pools and gently touch the waving tentacles of sea anemones, they stick to my fingers and sting a little. If I listen carefully, I hear the whoosh of wings pushing through the air as a raven flies past.

I've probably spent months of my life exploring beaches and tide pools, but there is always something new. One day I heard a low-level, constant, scraping noise. I looked around. No one else on the beach, no birds or large animals in sight. What could it be? It sounded like it was coming from the rocks, so I looked closer. Eventually I noticed that the barnacles themselves were moving. They were stuck to the rock, so they couldn't actually go anywhere, but hundreds of them were rotating in circles inside their shells. They appeared to be scraping the insides of their shells. I don't know why—perhaps to clean them or to make them bigger—but, amazingly, the sound came from their scraping.

I thought I knew barnacles. I grew up watching them eat, I'd done science experiments on them in school, and I know how to walk barefoot on them without cutting my feet. But this was new— I'd never heard them before. Now that I know what I am listening for, I have heard the barnacles again on different beaches. It amazes me every time.

Barnacles. JENS WIETING

CHAPTER THREE

People at the Edge of the Sea

Before immigrants came to BC from Europe, China, Russia and Hawaii, there were people living on the coast. These are the First Nations people. To this day they continue to live there, maintaining their own cultures, traditions and governments.

In the Great Bear Rainforest, all of the towns and villages face the water. The First Nations live at the edge between land and sea, as they have done since time before memory. Newcomers to the coast—the early settlers and more recent immigrants—also often choose to live along the water's edge.

"The intertidal zone is our dinner table. When the tide goes out, our table is set."
—**Gerald Amos**, Haisla First Nation (1949–)

OPPOSITE: The design on a First Nations button blanket signifies the family crest or clan of the person wearing it.
MIKE AMBACH

The First Peoples

There were people living all across North America for thousands of years before Europeans arrived. When Christopher Columbus first arrived in the Caribbean in 1492, he believed he had found the East Indies, so he called

Canoes pulled up on the
beach in front of Skidegate,
a town on Haida Gwaii, circa 1890.
IMAGE B-03660 COURTESY OF
ROYAL BC MUSEUM, BC ARCHIVES

the people who lived there Indians. But across Canada, the first peoples already had names for themselves. Today in BC, they prefer to be known as First Nations, to emphasize that there were nations here prior to European colonization. In other places, the first peoples refer to themselves as aboriginal, indigenous and native. The people in the Far North call themselves the Inuit.

All First Nations have a more specific name as well, in their own language. On BC's north coast, the Haisla are "the people who live at the mouth of the river." The people in Hartley Bay call themselves the Gitga'at, which means "people of the cane." They have that name because their original village site was up a river too shallow to paddle. They had to use "canes" or poles to push their canoes up the river to the village.

When Europeans first sailed up the west coast of North America, they gave English and Spanish names to the places they "discovered." But the First Nations already had names for these places. The islands off the north coast of BC that the Haida call home were named the Queen Charlotte

VOICES FROM THE COAST

Our food is not sold in stores
Morgan Hill (14), Gitga'at First Nation

"I like being able to see the ocean every morning when I wake up. I like watching whales and bears, and I enjoy going seagull-egg hunting. I like being able to hear animals instead of cars and alarms. I like how safe the coast is, and how small my village is, where you can walk by everyone and know who they are. I like being able to harvest all the traditional foods. If we couldn't gather it ourselves, we would have to buy what we could. But not much of the food we eat would ever be for sale."

Islands by a European fur trader in 1787. Today, the islands are once again known by their original name, Haida Gwaii, which means "Islands of the People."

The Roots Go Deep

Each First Nation on the coast of BC has a story or creation myth that explains how the world came to be. The Heiltsuk people on the central coast believe they were set down on their land by the Creator, along with gifts of stone, trees, houses, food, transportation, fire and companions. Some of the Haida say that Raven opened a clam shell and called for the people to come out.

At a place called Namu on BC's central coast, archaeologists found 9,000-year-old fishing gear. There is evidence of Heiltsuk habitation on the central coast going even further back. About 10,000 years ago, most of this coast was covered in thick ice. But there were places on Haida Gwaii and other parts of the coast that were never covered by ice and may have been home to First Nations people a very long time ago. Some of these early villages would have been flooded as the glaciers receded and sea levels rose.

As the glaciers retreated, trees and animals moved north. Where the ice had once been, forests now grew, fertilized by the spawning salmon. By about 5,000 years ago, the cedar, known as the "tree of life," became an integral part of the culture of west coast First Nations. And salmon were thick in the rivers. With all this ecological abundance, the people of the coast could dedicate time to art and culture.

First Nations built permanent villages with houses big enough to hold thirty to sixty people. Skilled artists carved massive totem poles that stood in front of the houses. People traveled around the coast in carved cedar canoes,

TAKE ACTION

Get to know your neighbors
If you are not aboriginal yourself, who are the First Nations or native people who have lived for thousands of years in the place you now call home? What language do (or did) they speak? Do they have any festivals or events that you could go to, as a way of getting to know them? Talk to people, ask questions, listen to their stories. Read books written by First Nations writers in your area, watch TV shows and movies made by aboriginal directors, with aboriginal actors.

If you are aboriginal, what are the stories of the immigrants who now share your home? Where did they come from and why did they leave their previous homes?

Dancing at a Haida feast. MIKE AMBACH

sometimes going distances of 1,500 kilometers (930 miles). Some of the canoes were so big they could hold more than forty people! First Nations held ceremonies called **potlatches** where they sang, gave gifts and danced with ceremonial masks.

Up and down the coast there were, and still are, many different First Nations. These nations traded with each other, went to war with each other, stole slaves from each other, made peace with each other and married each other. To this day, there are complex political relationships among the nations on the coast, and each retains its unique language, culture and traditions.

Cedar, the Tree of Life

Western red cedar is known as the tree of life because it offers so much to the people who live on the coast. Many different parts of the tree can be used: the wood, bark, roots and even the small branches. A great deal of skill, creativity and artistry goes into the harvesting, carving, weaving and working with cedar. These skills have been passed down from generation to generation.

Cedar bark can be stripped off the side of a tree without harming it. If the bark is soaked in water and then pounded to make it soft and bendable, it can be used to make woven baskets, bags, hats, rope, clothing and even waterproof containers for bailing water out of canoes.

Cedar wood has many special properties. It can be so easily split that it's possible to remove a large plank of wood from the side of a tree without damaging the tree. Wood that has been steamed can be bent to make boxes, bowls, cradles and drums. And the wood decays much more slowly than other types of wood, making it

First Nations of the
Great Bear Rainforest

Lax Kw'alaams
Metlakatla
Gitxaala   Haisla
Haida   Gitga'at
Kitasoo/
Xai'Xais
Nuxalk
Heiltsuk
Da'naxda'xw/Awaetlatla
Dzawada'enuxw   Wuikinuxv
Gwa'Sala Nakwaxda'xw
Gwa'wa'aineuk
Kwiakah
Kwiksutaineuk-ah-kwa-mish
Mamalilikulla-Que'Qwa'Sot'Em
Tlowitsis

MAP: These First Nations have called the Great Bear Rainforest home since time before memory.

a good choice for building homes and totem poles that can withstand all the rain in the rainforest.

Historically, tools for carving were made from stone and antlers. When Europeans arrived, tools were made from iron. What has stayed the same, though, is the shape of the tools, the techniques for carving and the way young carvers learn by apprenticing with a master carver.

Because the wood is so light, it can be carved into intricate ceremonial masks of birds, animals and supernatural beings. Some masks have long beaks that can be opened

OPPOSITE: Heiltsuk mask of a wild woman of the woods, seen here covering her mouth for a yawn.
QQS (EYES) PROJECTS SOCIETY

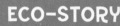

ECO-STORY

Feast day

When I step into a Heiltsuk big house on feast day, it's like entering another world, a world lit by firelight, where the boundaries between humans and spirits and animals dissolve. It is a place to glimpse and to experience the long rich history that First Nations have with this coast. I pause just inside the door to let my eyes adjust to the dim light. There is a fire burning in the center of the floor and a hole in the roof where the smoke goes out and some sunlight comes in. I notice the four carved house poles, one in each corner, that represent human and animal figures and signify our interconnectedness. As I make my way over to the wooden bleachers, where guests sit to watch the dancers, I notice the rich smell of the cedar wood used to build this place, mingled with the smell of smoke from the cedar burning on the fire.

At the end opposite the door there is a hollowed log with drummers lined up on either side. On cue they begin to sing and to drum on the log. As the big house fills with their voices, dancers wearing cedar headbands and button blankets enter and dance barefoot in the sand, all going the same direction around the fire. Each dance tells a story. Some dancers can make their hands flutter like wings, others bring to life the carved cedar masks they wear. Shafts of sunlight stream in through the smoky haze and light up the dancers. I feel honored to be invited into the big house to witness these dances.

Peeling cedar bark on Haida Gwaii.
ROBERT D. TURNER

TAKE ACTION

Learn your family history

If you are an aboriginal person, what is the history of your people? If you are not First Nations yourself, when did your family move to where you live now? Where did your grandparents and great-grandparents grow up? Were there aboriginal people where they lived? What was the relationship between settlers and aboriginal peoples like? What is it like now? Learn your own family stories.

and shut by the dancer. These masks are not carved to be displayed on a shelf in a museum—they are carved to be danced! A mask is best seen through the firelight and smoky haze inside a cedar-plank big house, in a dance that tells a story, accompanied by singing and drumming.

Arrival of the Europeans

In 1774, a Spanish ship sailed up the coast of BC. Without even coming ashore, the sailors claimed the region for Spain. A few years later, a British ship got lost in the fog and ended up on Vancouver Island. Someone jumped off the ship, stuck a flag in the ground and declared that the island was now under the control of the British Empire. For over a decade Britain and Spain argued about who owned this far-off land.

Meanwhile, the First Nations people were already here. Visitors from Russia had been trading with them for decades. And people from Asia, Hawaii and the west coast of North America had been crisscrossing the Pacific Ocean in both directions for hundreds, if not thousands, of years. When the Europeans arrived, the newcomers claimed the land for their own without asking permission from the people who lived there. Almost no treaties have been signed in BC, meaning that most of the First Nations never formally agreed to share their land.

Europeans brought metal tools, which they traded with the First Nations for sea otter furs. First Nations were skilled traders, and the new tools made carving easier. But the Europeans brought something else with them also: disease. Smallpox devastated the populations of coastal communities, because the aboriginal people had little immunity to this foreign disease. So many people died that whole villages were abandoned. There weren't even enough people left alive to properly bury the dead.

A Great Injustice

To give immigrants somewhere to live, the government of the day had to find a way to move aboriginal peoples off the land. First Nations were informed that they could now only live within small **Indian reserves** that had been mapped out by government officials. The government was then able to sell the rest of the land to immigrants, to live on and build their farms.

Heiltsuk youth paddling a big canoe, south of Bella Bella.
QQS (EYES) PROJECTS SOCIETY

But the way First Nations tell the story, they saw their land being taken away from them. With the land went their ability to provide for themselves and to feed their children. The reserves they were told to live on were too small to provide food or jobs. In the 1880s, Tsimshian

VOICES FROM THE COAST

Stories from our ancestors

Kii'iljuus Barbara Wilson, Haida First Nation

Barbara lives on Haida Gwaii and shares stories from her Haida ancestors.

"We have lived on our land since it was neither light nor dark, they say. Our ancestors, the supernatural beings, came from the ocean and could shape-shift (or change) from ocean creatures to humans at will. They left stories for us telling of a time when at least two floods came to our world, when volcanoes, earthquakes and ice came, how we had to leave the islands, and then how we eventually returned from the south. Our stories talk about a time when the salt water was one hundred and forty meters lower and the area between Haida Gwaii and the mainland was grasslands, with small pines and sedges. It was cold and no large trees existed on the land yet."

chiefs from the north coast paddled all the way (more than 1,000 kilometers, or 600 miles) down to Victoria, the province's capital, to protest how their land had been taken away. When they weren't listened to in Victoria, they traveled even farther, this time to Ottawa, to try and be heard. Some went as far as England to talk directly with the Queen. But it didn't help. By the year 1900, most of the Indian reserves in BC had been established, and they were small. In total, all the Indian reserves in BC make up less than half of 1 percent of the province.

As the First Nations were moved off their land, saw their children taken away and had their cultural and

OPPOSITE:
First Nations gather in Mission to protest the small size of land they are expected to live on, circa 1900.
IMAGE G-00243 COURTESY OF ROYAL BC MUSEUM, BC ARCHIVES

VOICES FROM THE COAST

Dancing in the big house
Danielle Humchitt (15), Heiltsuk First Nation

The Heiltsuk run a summer science and culture camp at a place called Koeye (Kvai) on the central coast, where the Koeye River meets the ocean, and grizzly bears roam the white sandy beaches. Danielle has been coming to camp almost every summer since she was seven years old.

"I want to come to Koeye to learn more about our culture, and to learn new dances in the big house. I like it here because it's a home away from home. Koeye brings everyone closer together, and you make new friends. I like swimming, seeing the bears, and there are no cars here...Dancing is the best part about camp. Dancing in the big house makes you feel stronger.

"Feast day teaches kids how to be respectful in a real potlatch, and it shows you how powerful all the dances are. I am proud we have a Heiltsuk camp like this. It's important to have our elders teach the young to keep our culture going. People who went to **residential schools** can't speak the language, so it's important to bring our culture back. Salmon are an important part of feast day. We eat salmon, and also there is a salmon dance. It is for twins, but other people dance it also."

political traditions banned, they also witnessed the harvesting and depletion of the plants and animals they depended on. Settlers assumed that all the fish, fur and timber were theirs for the taking. Trees were logged to clear land for agriculture and to have lumber for buildings. Salmon were caught in large numbers, packed into tins at canneries up and down the coast, and shipped to England. The whales were hunted for their oil until there were hardly any left. Forced to live on small reserves, often the only way to survive was for the First Nations people to get work in the forestry industry, or to go fishing and sell salmon to the canneries. In this way, the First Nations also played a role in the depletion of the very things they depended on.

Eventually, things started to change. At no point had First Nations passively accepted all of the changes that were imposed on them. They spoke up, they protested, they lobbied political representatives. Some of the settlers were sympathetic, but it took years of organizing and court cases before First Nations got some of their rights back. In 1960, they were able for the first time to vote in federal elections. But it wasn't until 2001 that First Nations in the Great Bear Rainforest were finally recognized as governments with the authority and the right to make decisions about land use.

Where Did the Settlers Come From?

Throughout history, people moved to BC from around the world because they saw an opportunity to make a good living, or because they were forced to leave someplace else.

DID YOU KNOW

Taken from their families

In the late 1800s and throughout much of the 1900s, children were removed from First Nations communities and sent to live at residential schools. By 1896, fifteen hundred children from all of the First Nations across BC were living at these schools, cut off from their families and their culture. Children from the Great Bear Rainforest were sent to schools throughout BC—Port Alberni, Alert Bay, Chilliwack, Williams Lake, Lytton and Kamloops—and even as far away as Edmonton, Alberta. At the schools the students were punished for singing their family's songs, practicing their own religion and speaking their own languages. Many young children tried to run away, and not all survived. Those who eventually returned home had a hard time fitting in— they had forgotten their language, didn't know their cultural traditions and hadn't learned to hunt or fish. Nor had they learned the skills needed to get work among the settlers. To this day, the legacy of the residential schools affects the lives of many First Nations people.

DID YOU KNOW

Banning the potlatch

In 1884, the potlatch was banned by the government of Canada. A potlatch is a sacred cultural feast that can go on for days. Stories are told, masks are danced and the host family gives gifts to everyone who attends. The wealth and status of the host family is judged not by how much they have but by how much they give away. Potlatches are held to mark major events like births, deaths, the transfer of names and other important community business. These gatherings are so important to First Nations that even after they were banned, people would travel great distances to hold potlatches in secret. Those who got caught were put in jail, and their ceremonial masks were taken away and sold to museums. It wasn't until 1951 that First Nations were legally able to hold potlatches once again.

A potlatch in Klemtu. DOUGLAS NEASLOSS

In a piece of history repeated around the world and through the ages, people displaced from their homes moved somewhere new and, in turn, displaced the inhabitants who were already there. For example, in the eighteenth and nineteenth centuries over a million people had no choice but to leave their homes in Scotland, England and Ireland. Changing agricultural practices, the privatization of common land, and famine forced villagers to leave the land they had been farming for generations. No longer able to farm and with nowhere else to go, many of the displaced made the long journey to the colonies in North America.

In the early years, most settlers worked for the Hudson's Bay Company in the fur trading business. In the mid-1800s, people came in search of gold and to build a railway. When the gold ran out, immigrants came to farm and to work in the canneries.

Settlers came from Europe, China, Japan and Hawaii. To be able to talk to each other and to the local First Nations people, they created a new language called **Chinook Jargon**. It was spoken at fish canneries and among fur traders. For the most part the language died out with the end of the fur trade, but a few words still linger on. *Saltchuck* was the word for "ocean," and *skookum* meant "strong and brave."

After the First and Second World Wars in Europe, many people moved to Canada to start new lives far from the trenches, battlefields, bombed-out cities and concentration camps. There was work to be found in forestry, agriculture, fisheries and mining. These days, people continue to immigrate to Canada from all over the world in search of new opportunities and in hopes of a better life. Some arrive as refugees, fleeing countries where their religion, lifestyle or political beliefs put their lives at risk. All of us who live in Canada, except for the First Nations, are immigrants to this land. Someone in our family, maybe recently or maybe a long time ago, knows how it feels to step off a boat or a plane onto Canadian soil for the very first time.

Still Here, Still Dancing

Ever since Europeans first settled on this coast, First Nations have continuously voiced opposition to the way their land was taken away and how they have not been treated with respect. These days, their voices are finally starting to be heard. The highest level of court in Canada has recognized that First Nations have rights to the land, and the BC government has started to treat First Nations as governments also.

Despite all of the efforts to force First Nations people to be more like non-aboriginal Canadians, First Nations have survived along with their languages and cultures. There are ongoing challenges. After being disconnected from their land, sent to residential schools and subjected to ongoing discrimination, First Nations have higher levels of unemployment, lower incomes, higher suicide rates and a shorter life expectancy than the rest of the Canadian population. The fish and the forests they depend on for food and livelihood have been depleted. But the people on the coast are bringing their culture back. Dances and languages and other ancient traditions are being passed from elders to youth, instilling in them a sense of pride in their culture and a sense of community.

TOP: Workers building the Canadian Pacific Railway, 1885.
IMAGE C-00618 COURTESY OF ROYAL BC MUSEUM, BC ARCHIVES

BOTTOM: Posing with masks and regalia outside the big house at Koeye, where Heiltsuk youth learn the songs and dances of their culture.
QQS (EYES) PROJECTS SOCIETY

CHAPTER FOUR

From Pseudoscorpions to Grizzly Bears

B efore you read any further, get a piece of paper and draw a picture of your favorite tree. Okay, now look at your picture. What kind of tree is it? Did you draw just the tree above ground or did you also draw the roots? Most people, when asked to draw a tree, only draw the parts that we can see: the trunk and branches and leaves. But did you know that half of a tree is actually below the ground? It makes sense when you stop to think about it—how else would a giant tree keep itself from falling over? Roots are also important because they are how a tree gets water and nutrients from the soil.

"It's not that we can make a difference. It's that we do make a difference."
—Julia Butterfly Hill, American environmental activist (1974–)

OPPOSITE: Gazing up at a big Sitka spruce tree can make a person feel small. TJ WATT

Walking into an Old-Growth Forest

Imagine you have just stepped off the boat onto the beach or rocky shoreline, and the trees of the Great Bear Rainforest loom up in front of you, tall and green.

DID YOU KNOW

A special little frog

Frogs are **amphibians**, spending part of their lives in the water and part on land. There is a special little frog called the coastal tailed frog that lives only in the coastal temperate rainforest. These tiny frogs live in cool, fast-flowing mountain streams and in the adjacent old-growth forests. When frogs emerge from their eggs, they have tails and no legs and are called tadpoles. At this stage in their life, they swim around in water; only later do they grow the legs that allow them to move onto dry ground. Because coastal tailed frog tadpoles live in fast-flowing streams, they have adapted sucker devices so they can attach themselves to rocks and not get washed downstream. As adults, coastal tailed frogs have almost no lungs and breathe mainly through their skin. They live for fifteen to twenty years, making them one of the longest-lived frogs in the world.

Coastal tailed frog. JARED HOBBS

The salal bushes are so thick you might need to get down on your hands and knees and crawl underneath to get through. As you leave the beach and move into the forest, pay attention to what you see, feel and hear.

First of all, notice how the temperature changes as you go into the shade of the forest. In the summer it's cooler under the trees than it is on the beach. (In winter the opposite is true because the forest provides shelter from the winter storms.) Notice the damp, woodsy smell, kind of like the smell of wet soil when you are digging in a garden or walking in a park after a rain. If you are quiet, you might hear birds rustling in the bushes and an eagle singing from a tree branch high overhead. Eagles often sit on branches right beside the water, where they can keep an eye out for fish.

It's hard not to stare at Sitka spruce trees that are over 2 meters (6.6 feet) wide and 30 meters (98 feet) tall. That is as tall as a nine-story building! In some river valleys in the Great Bear Rainforest, the trees grow more than twice as big, up to 80 meters (295 feet) tall. The trees are so tall that you have to crane your head way back, and then back some more, to see where the treetops touch the sky.

These ancient trees are awe-inspiring, but soon your neck will need a rest. When you decide to continue your exploring, you'll find it's hard to walk anywhere because there are thick bushes and massive fallen logs all over the place.

As you clamber through the forest, you can see trees of all different ages. There are mosses and lichens and even ferns growing on the trunks of the older trees.

If you look carefully, you might find grizzly bear hair that's been rubbed off onto the bark of a tree. Bears do this to mark their territory. There are berry bushes and small white flowers called foamflower and bunchberry that grow really close to the ground. Everywhere you look, there are more shades of green than you can count, no matter what time of year it is.

But what is happening below the forest floor? Your feet land on deep mossy mats, and you are constantly stepping over logs lying on the ground. The surface is uneven and soft and it holds a whole world of biodiversity under our feet.

More Than Just Dirt

Soil plays a key role in any forest. And even though you can't see it unless you look closely, what happens beneath your feet can be fascinating. Soil is formed when rocks are ground down over time by heat, water or wind (or even by the **fungi** in lichens or attached to tree roots) into tiny grains

TAKE ACTION

Play with dirt!
What is the soil like where you live? Look at it under a microscope (a dissecting microscope is best) and compare soil from an old-growth forest with soil from a **second-growth forest**. Or compare soil from your schoolyard with soil from a park. What are the differences? Around the world, the layer of soil called **topsoil** is the most valuable to farmers, because it is the best soil to grow crops in. Dig a hole to find out how deep the topsoil is. You'll know you've reached the bottom of the topsoil when the dark layer ends and you start digging into lighter-colored soil.

ABOVE: When a tree falls in the forest...it's still part of the forest.
ANDREW S. WRIGHT

LEFT: Sleeping grizzly bear cub. DOUGLAS NEASLOSS

of sand, silt and clay, and then combined with the remains of plants and animals that have died and decomposed.

All kinds of little creatures live in the soil, and they play an important role in decomposing the decaying plants into something that the trees can use for food. Some of these you might know well, such as slugs and beetles. Millipedes shred plant material, beginning the decomposition process. One species contains cyanide, which smells like almonds but is poison·to any potential predators. Many of these creatures are so tiny that you need a microscope to see them. Some of these **microorganisms** look so fantastical it's hard to believe they are real. Pseudoscorpions look a lot like miniature scorpions (but without the stinger). Nematodes, a kind of microscopic worm, eat bacteria and fungi and help make nutrients available to plants. Springtails are

OPPOSITE (TOP): Mushrooms growing on the forest floor. JENS WIETING

OPPOSITE (BOTTOM): A ground beetle on a salmon carcass. MORGAN HOCKING

VOICES FROM THE COAST

The raven and the spirit bear
Douglas Neasloss, Kitasoo/Xai'xais First Nation

Douglas is a bear-viewing guide from the Kitasoo/Xai'xais First Nation. He lives in Klemtu on the central coast.

"I have a lot of respect for all bears, but the white bear certainly demands a bit more attention. The white bear is important to me because of its uniqueness. To me and to a lot of my people, there almost seems to be something magical about it. I have seen hundreds of bears over the course of ten years as a guide and am still in awe when I see the spirit bear.

"We have a story about Wee'get the Raven making every tenth black bear white. The raven is known as the creator in our culture, and he created the ice age. When the ice started to melt, he wanted something to remind him of the ice age, so he made every tenth black bear white as a reminder of when the world was covered in ice and snow. He set these rare bears on Princess Royal Island to be their home, and the island was to be protected for all time where they could live in peace."

less than 6 millimeters (0.2 inches) long but have the ability to jump several centimeters. Imagine jumping five times your own height! Springtails chew on decomposing plants and fungi, and there are a lot of them in the soil.

When a bear leaves a salmon on the forest floor, these tiny creatures help to decompose it into something a tree can use. A tree cannot survive without the help of all this activity in the soil. The forest depends on these insects, fungi and bacteria to decompose leaves and make nutrients available for plants and trees.

Not all the critters in the soil eat plants; there are predators among them. Some mites scavenge leaves and rotten wood. Other mites are more aggressive; they feed on nematodes, insect larvae and other mites and spring-tails. Pseudoscorpions seize their victims with their front claws and then inject poison from the tips of the claws. Their **prey** includes nematodes, mites, and larvae.

Fun Facts About Fungi

The identity of the world's largest living **organism** might surprise you. It's not a blue whale or an ancient tree. In fact, it's something you can barely see, because most of it is underground and microscopic. The world's largest living organism is a fungus in the state of Oregon that covers over 965 hectares (2,384 acres, or an area the size of 1,665 football fields) and is estimated to be at least 2,400 years old but is possibly much older.

What is a fungus? Fungi (the plural of fungus) are neither plant nor animal. Fungi include mushrooms, truffles, yeasts and molds. The antibiotic penicillin is made from a fungus.

TOP: Bunchberry, a small plant that grows on the forest floor. JENS WIETING

BOTTOM: A waterfall washes soil from the steep slope, exposing the bedrock. DOUGLAS NEASLOSS

OPPOSITE: Ancient, giant, fallen cedar tree. TJ WATT

But the giant fungus in Oregon isn't a massive mushroom! Mostly, the only parts of fungi that we see are the mushrooms that sprout up from the ground or from rotting logs. In fact, most of the fungi are underground. They form delicate root-like threads, collectively called **mycelium**, that spread through the soil. If you were to measure all the thin threads of mycelium found in a shovelful of rainforest soil they would stretch out for kilometers.

Some fungi are harmful and will kill trees. Other fungi are extremely helpful. In the coastal temperate rainforest, **mycorrhizal fungi** form **mutually beneficial** relationships with tree roots. This means that both the fungi and the trees are getting something good out of their association with one another. The fungal mycelium attaches to tree roots and spreads out into the surrounding soil. Without the mycelium, the trees couldn't absorb all the water and minerals they need to grow. And in return, the fungi get sugars that the trees produce. Both the trees and the fungi depend on this partnership for their survival. Old-growth Douglas-firs may have up to forty different kinds of mycorrhizal fungus attached to their root systems. And each fungus is attached to multiple trees. Probably each tree in a forest is connected to other trees, and can exchange nutrients with other trees, through this network of fungi. There are an estimated three thousand species of fungus at work in the soils of the coastal temperate rainforest.

Deeper into the Forest

As you walk farther into the forest, you notice that some trees grow from the ground, while others grow out of old stumps or fallen logs. These fallen logs are called "**nurse logs**," because they provide the right habitat for certain plants and trees to grow. Huckleberries grow best on nurse logs and are eaten by bears, birds and people. Birds play an important role in distributing berry seeds throughout the forest. Can you guess how they do this? If you guessed that they eat the berries and then poop out the seeds in other parts of the forest, you're right! Hemlock trees also like to grow on nurse logs. Eventually, after a very long time, nurse logs turn into soil.

Fallen, decaying logs are also a good place to find insects, and that is just where bears look for them. Sometimes you'll find an old log that a bear has ripped apart, digging around for bugs to eat.

It's a Bear's Life

You might think that if you were a big bear you wouldn't need to worry about anything. But that isn't the case. If a grizzly bear comes across a black bear, the black bear will

ECO-STORY

Strange playmates

If you want to see wildlife, the best times of day are dawn and dusk, because that's when the animals are most active. One day at dusk I was in the Great Bear Rainforest in the Bella Coola Valley. A fox suddenly ran into the field in front of me, followed by a deer. Wait a minute. Was the deer really following the fox? The fox scampered about playfully, flopped down on the ground and looked back at the deer expectantly. The deer followed. The fox went around a tree and the deer went around the same tree. And then they both went around the tree again. Eventually they moved off across the field, the fox darting about, the deer following steadily. In this magical moment I was reminded that there are connections between species that we don't expect or understand.

DID YOU KNOW

Bear trails

In some areas, grizzlies make what are called bear trails, where they have been taking the exact same paths for so long that their steps have left permanent markings in the moss. Each time a bear walks on its trail, it puts its feet in *exactly* the same places!

"If you are a poet, you will see clearly that there is a cloud floating in this sheet of paper. Without a cloud, there will be no rain; without rain, the trees cannot grow; and without trees, we cannot make paper...If we look into this sheet of paper even more deeply, we can see the sunshine in it. Without sunshine, the forest cannot grow...And if we continue to look, we can see the logger who cut the tree and brought it to the mill to be transformed into paper. And we see wheat. We know that the logger cannot exist without his daily bread, and therefore the wheat that became his bread is also in this sheet of paper. The logger's father and mother are in it too. When we look in this way, we see that without all of these things, this sheet of paper cannot exist."

—**Thich Nhat Hanh,**
Vietnamese Buddhist monk (1926–)
(from *The Heart of Understanding: Commentaries on the Prajnaparamita Sutra* [1988] by Thich Nhat Hanh, reprinted with permission of Parallax Press, Berkeley, California)

leave or climb a tree to get out of the way. And all bears will run from a pack of wolves! Wolves truly are the top predator in the coastal rainforest and can easily attack and kill a bear. Life as a bear isn't all that easy after all.

A bear needs to eat a huge amount to survive. Bears eat plants, bugs, berries and salmon. I once saw a black bear sitting on its rump, hind legs spread out on either side of a berry bush, stuffing its face with wild blueberries. Bears spend more time eating plants than fish, but they need salmon in order to fatten up before their long winter hibernation. They especially like the eggs from inside female salmon that are about to spawn. Grizzly bears will lick up salmon eggs from the gravel, flicking them with their tongues into their mouths. These eggs are so rich in nutrients that it is worth the time it takes for these big animals to eat the tiny eggs one by one.

We Are All Connected

In an ecosystem, big things depend on small things and small things depend on big things. A huge bear eating tiny eggs is one example of how everything is connected in the rainforest. Plants and animals need each other, because nothing in this world exists completely on its own.

In the Great Bear Rainforest the bears drag salmon into the forest, where insects and fungi turn the salmon into food for the trees, which then provide homes to birds in their branches and to wolves in dens under their roots. When a tree falls over in a big windstorm, berry bushes grow on the fallen tree and insects decompose the wood. Bears eat the berries and also insects such as ants and termites that live in the fallen log. Sometimes wolves eat bears, but mostly they eat salmon and the deer that live among the big trees. People also eat salmon and deer, and use the bark and wood of the cedar trees. Changes to one part of this ecosystem, even a small part, have consequences for everything else. Our future cannot be separated from the future of the insects of the soil and the frogs and salmon of the rainforest.

TAKE ACTION

Breathing with a plant
Go outside and sit down beside a plant. It doesn't matter what kind: a rose, an apple tree, a fern...Put your face close to a leaf and just breathe, in and out. With each breath out you exhale carbon dioxide onto the leaf, which absorbs it. And then when you inhale, you breathe in the oxygen that the plant gives off. To be able to breathe, you need the plant. And it needs you. Think about how you are breathing with a plant.

OPPOSITE: A spirit bear fishes for salmon in the rain. DOUGLAS NEASLOSS

ECO-STORY

Witness to an attack

One day at university I had the chance to look at soil under a special microscope. It was soil from an old-growth coastal temperate rainforest. I was supposed to be counting the number of insects I could see. But two mites were attacking a nematode, and I couldn't pull my eyes away. The nematode was much bigger than both of the mites combined, but they were holding on while the nematode writhed around. Meanwhile, lurking in the shadows, a pseudoscorpion was hiding under a pine needle. So much drama, right under our feet.

CHAPTER FIVE

Fish and Fur

Looking to the Past

If you live in a place where all the old-growth forests have been logged, you might think that trees don't get very big. If the trees around you are all less than one or two hundred years old, you might think that is as tall and wide as they get. To know what healthy ecosystems used to look like, and to measure the changes that have occurred, we need to find and learn about existing old-growth forests. We need to look as far back as possible and listen to the stories of how things used to be. Only from knowing the past can we assess what actions need to be taken today to protect or restore ecosystems.

What are the stories from the Great Bear Rainforest? What did it used to be like compared to what it's like now? What has been harvested from the forest and the surrounding ocean? What is still there?

"I am only one, but still I am one. I cannot do everything, but still I can do something. Because I cannot do everything, I will not refuse to do the something that I can do."
—Edward Everett Hale, American author (1822–1909)

OPPOSITE: A spirit bear looks for salmon in the river. ANDREW S. WRIGHT

Fishermen's dock,
McTavish Cannery, Rivers Inlet, 1920.
IMAGE H-06492 COURTESY OF
ROYAL BC MUSEUM, BC ARCHIVES

TAKE ACTION

Sharing the stories

Ask your grandparents or other elders in your community to tell you what the land was like when they were young. Or you can find this out from books. Did there used to be a forest closer to your town or city than there is now, and were the trees bigger or smaller than they are today? What about the animals, and the fish in the rivers? What do your elders say has changed in their lifetime? What do they think about the changes? Listening to the stories, and then sharing them with others, can inspire people to take action to protect ecosystems they care about.

Fish So Thick You Could Walk on Water

Old fishermen say that when the salmon gathered at the mouths of rivers, they were so thick that you could practically walk across the river on the backs of all the fish. There were so many millions of fish that the rivers looked black. Ravens were so full from eating salmon that they couldn't even fly.

The First Nations people have been harvesting salmon on this coast for thousands of years. In the past, First Nations used wooden and stone fish traps to catch the salmon. With their technology, they were capable of wiping out all the salmon. But they didn't. And it wasn't because they had fewer mouths to feed. In fact, First Nations caught as many salmon per year as were caught, on average, by the commercial salmon fishery in the twentieth century. But they did this in such a way that the salmon came back year after year. How? Guided by respect for the creatures that brought the gift of food each year, they showed restraint. They waited a few days once the salmon arrived before starting to fish; they took their traps out of the water to allow salmon up the river to spawn; and sometimes they built traps with holes in them so a few salmon could always get through. The First Nations understood that there would be no salmon in the future if enough salmon weren't allowed to swim upstream. Also, the First Nations caught salmon in the rivers or the mouths of rivers, where it was always possible to ensure that enough salmon were left to spawn. In contrast, the modern-day fishery catches salmon in the ocean. A school of salmon caught in a big net might contain all the fish headed to a specific stream, leaving none left to spawn.

As writer Terry Glavin puts it, First Nations managed their fisheries with the understanding that "if you screw up, you starve to death." Modern-day fishing has been guided by the principle that "if you screw up, you open a cannery farther up the coast, or you go into a different industry." The attitude toward salmon shifted from seeing them as a life-sustaining resource to seeing them as a profit-making opportunity. The consequences of that shift in attitude are what we are living with today.

When European immigrants first settled on the Pacific coast, the rivers were full of fish. But early settlers were more interested in the furs, the trees and the gold. It wasn't until someone figured out how to process and store salmon in cans that settlers became interested in fishing.

The salmon canning industry began in California and quickly spread north to BC. By 1900 there were seventy-eight canneries operating along the BC coast, and more quickly followed. Canned salmon was shipped to England, where it was sold as cheap food to factory workers. In the early days of the canning industry, fishing boats were small and the fish were never in short supply. Rivers Inlet in the Great Bear Rainforest was lined with canneries, and there were so many boats that people said you could cross the inlet by stepping from boat to boat. The demand for salmon by the canneries put pressure on the fishery to develop new technologies so that more salmon could be caught faster. By around 1910, motorized boats with bigger nets could intercept entire schools

DID YOU KNOW

Working in a cannery

Each cannery was an **assembly line** where thousands of cans of salmon were **mass-produced**. The salmon had to be put into cans within a few hours of being caught so that the fish didn't go bad. The workers were expected to work quickly, and their days were long.

Typically, canneries were owned by Europeans, while most of the workers were Chinese, Japanese and First Nations. In the early days, the different jobs in a cannery were divided up on a racial basis. Probably this was intended to maintain divisions among workers and discourage anyone from organizing and demanding higher wages. Chinese men made the cans by hand. First Nations men, and later also the Japanese, did the fishing. Chinese men unloaded fish from the boats and butchered them. Some of these men could butcher four or five large fish a minute, taking out the guts and cutting off the fins. Aboriginal and Japanese women washed the fish and filled the cans, packing as many as three cans per minute. Chinese men closed and cooked the cans, labeled them and put them into cases for transport. The people of European descent acted mostly as managers and bookkeepers, and were often paid more than four times what the non-white workers were paid.

Packing cans with salmon, Ceepeecee Cannery, 1946.
IMAGE I-26242 COURTESY OF ROYAL BC MUSEUM, BC ARCHIVES

of salmon. So many salmon were caught that by the 1940s catches were starting to decline.

These days, the canneries are abandoned ruins along the coast, their old wooden buildings slowly sinking into the sea. Commercial fishing boats have onboard refrigeration, so they can transport all the fish to centralized fish-processing plants in Vancouver and Prince Rupert. But even the commercial fishing boats are few and far between. In part this is because each boat is so big, and the technology so efficient, that it's possible to catch large numbers of fish without many

VOICES FROM THE COAST

"The Eulachon Lady"
Megan Moody, Nuxalk First Nation

Megan remembers catching eulachon with her bare hands. Megan is a member of the Nuxalk Nation and grew up in Bella Coola. In the Nuxalk language, the word for eulachon is *sputc* (pronounced "spooth"). When she was a kid in the 1980s, the eulachon were all over the place. She remembers watching eulachon grease being made at the stink pit, and she says it was a fun time of year. The Nuxalk word for grease is *sluq'* (pronounced "slook"). All the kids and elders would gather together, stories would be told, and everyone seemed happy and excited as they made the grease.

While Megan was away at school, the eulachon stopped returning. Just like that! When she returned home in 2001, she was shocked to find there were still no eulachon. Each year since then, everyone keeps hoping the fish will come back.

Megan decided that she could help by doing research. Her goal is to solve the mystery of why the eulachon disappeared and how to get them back.

For Megan, it is a huge thing to be helping her community. Everywhere she goes in Bella Coola, people call her the "eulachon lady" and ask her if the fish are returning. Megan worries that the younger Nuxalk kids don't know what eulachon taste like or how special they are, and she doesn't want this knowledge to be lost. Her dream is to once again see her people fishing for eulachon along the banks of the river.

people or boats. But there are also fewer fishing boats out on the water because there are fewer fish.

Up and down the coast, people are talking about salmon—how many there used to be, and what little is left. Salmon are the life blood of the rainforest, transporting nutrients from the ocean up the rivers for the bears, the wolves, the people and even the trees. Without salmon the ecosystem feels hollow and gutted, on the brink of collapse.

Eulachon: The Candlefish

It used to be that the rivers of the central and north coast were black with eulachon (sometimes spelled oolichan and pronounced "oo-li-kan") in the spring. In Bella Coola, there were so many eulachon that they spilled onto the gravel bars beside the river. They looked like big black clouds of fish, and you could catch them with your hands. Since 1999, the river has been almost empty of fish. What happened?

Eulachon are small fish that live in the ocean but return to the rivers to lay their eggs, just like salmon do. Sea lions, seals and even whales will sometimes follow schools of eulachon into estuaries and up rivers. They are the first fish to return to the rivers after the long winter, which makes them an important food for First Nations.

Eulachon are good to eat, but they have many other uses also. A dried eulachon is so oily that it can be burned like a candle! The oil from eulachon, known as "grease," is collected by fermenting the fish in big vats called "stink boxes," cooking the aged fish, and then scooping the oil off the top. The grease is eaten, traded and used as both a medicine and a food preservative. The Nuxalk, for example, traded eulachon grease for herring eggs and seaweed from the Heiltsuk, who didn't have any eulachon

TAKE ACTION

Do research to learn more
One of the first actions you can take when you hear or see something that concerns you is to learn more about it. You can go online, go to a library or a bookstore, or talk to people who are involved. With more information, you will be better prepared to decide what further action to take.

DID YOU KNOW ?

Fish stories

People like to brag about the biggest fish they ever caught. The biggest salmon on record was a 57-kilogram (126-pound) Chinook salmon that was 135 centimeters (53 inches) long. It was caught in Petersburg, Alaska, in 1949. Halibut are large bottom-fish that swim along the ocean floor, eating whatever fish they can find. In the 1930s in Alaska, a halibut was caught that weighed 225 kilograms (495 pounds). Think about how much you weigh, and then imagine how big these fish were. Most of the fish caught these days are much smaller than these, but people still dream of catching a big one! Maybe one day the big ones can come back.

in their area. And the Nuxalk traded the grease with First Nations who lived in the interior of BC. The trails used for trading between the coast and the interior were so well used they were called "grease trails."

But for the last twelve years in the spring along the central coast, the eulachon haven't come back to the rivers. Everyone is waiting for them. The people are waiting, and so are the seals, the seagulls, the geese, the otters and the wolves...

Why the eulachon disappeared so fast is a bit of a mystery. The eulachon were being affected by many things: pollution, logging practices that damaged spawning habitat, changing water temperature, an increased abundance of predators due to climate change, and a shrimp trawl fishery that unintentionally caught huge numbers of eulachon while fishing for shrimp. One of these factors, or a combination of all of them, was the final straw, and in central coast rivers the population of eulachon dropped so low that they have not been able to recover. Eulachon still return to a few northern rivers. In 2010 the Skeena and the Nass rivers had good numbers of eulachon returning. But on most parts of the coast, people are worried about the eulachon and are unsure what they can do to bring them back.

Abalone

Abalone (pronounced "ah-baloney") are small creatures with one big foot and a multicolored iridescent shell. They like to live on rocky shorelines, especially where there is a lot of seaweed. Their favorite food is kelp (a kind of seaweed), and they have to compete for food with the sea urchins, who usually win. Abalone have to watch out that they don't become a meal for octopus, crab, lobsters, sea stars and otters. Apparently their muscular foot is very tasty. Abalone used to be an important part of the diet of First Nations. Today, there are not enough abalone left to harvest even a few for ceremonial purposes. What happened?

In the 1960s, scuba diving was invented. A diver could take a basket underwater and scoop large numbers of abalone off the rocks. In the 1970s, abalone from BC began to be sold in Japan, and people could sell as much as they were able to harvest. Over the years, abalone were over-harvested and lots of money was made. It became harder and harder to find them. Today, there are so few left that it is illegal to fish for abalone.

Where Did the Whales Go?

When Europeans first settled the land now called British Columbia, one of the big businesses was hunting whales. Whales were hunted for their oil and the comb-like structures called **baleen** that some whales have in their mouths to filter food. Whale oil was used in factories. In 1851, one cotton mill required the oil from three sperm whales—25,635 liters (6,772 gallons)—just to keep the factory running for a single year. Baleen was used by the garment industry for hoop skirts, corsets and shirt collars.

In the beginning, right whales were the preferred species because they produced more oil than other whales and because they didn't sink when they were killed. But by the 1890s there were so few right whales in the North Pacific Ocean that the whalers started hunting other species. The population of right whales has never recovered. In 2010 there were only thirty right whales left in

TOP: A sunflower sea star (the largest sea star in the world) chases an abalone. THOMAS P. PESCHAK

BOTTOM: Humpback whale breaches (jumps) out of the water before landing with a splash. DOUGLAS NEASLOSS

OPPOSITE: A 136-kilogram (300-pound) halibut, Alaska, 1910. ALASKA STATE LIBRARY

the eastern North Pacific, off the coast of Alaska. It is possibly the world's smallest whale population, and it is not expected to survive.

The story of gray whales is a more positive one. Before whaling began, it is estimated that there were around 24,000 gray whales off the western coast of North America. By the early 1900s, most had been hunted and there were only 2,000 left. But the gray whales have come back. They were legally protected from hunting in 1946 and have recovered to their original numbers. Each spring, thousands

VOICES FROM THE COAST

The taste of abalone

Lynne Hill, Gitga'at First Nation

Lynne is a teacher at the school in Hartley Bay. She wrote a story about the taste of abalone, about remembering the past and being worried for the future.

"My granddaughter Morgan has lived all her life in Hartley Bay. She is part of the Gitga'at people. Morgan's feast name is Lax Gyoos wil KIgul bilhaa, and it means "Abalone have their babies on the kelp." But most people just call her Morgan.

"One day in school Morgan's teacher asked the students, 'How many of you have tasted abalone?' Morgan knew that abalone was an animal that lived on the rocks in the water and that the shells were beautiful rainbow colors. But she had never tasted one! Her great-grandmother told her that long ago they used to be able to get abalone by the sackful, and that they were delicious. She said that they were good raw and, if you were going to cook them, that you had to pound them first and then fry them and eat them with rice. But Morgan had never tasted one.

"Morgan and I worry that in the future kids won't know the taste of clams either. We want everyone to plan for the future so that when a teacher asks the kids if they have ever tasted a clam, the answer won't be No."

Adapted with permission from *"Tell me again!" By one of us who remembers and who is worried.* © 2007 Lynne Hill

of gray whales can be seen traveling up the coast from their winter breeding grounds off Baja California to their summer feeding grounds in northern waters. Baby whales, called calves, can be seen swimming close to their mothers. They are evidence that recovery is possible, and they inspire hope for the future.

Fur Frenzy

Sea otters are different than other marine mammals. Instead of the thick layers of blubber that keep seals and whales warm in the cold ocean, sea otters have fur. They have the warmest fur coats of any animal in the world. This is because they have more hairs in a square centimeter of fur (150,000 hairs) than most humans have on their entire head (100,000 hairs)!

Before the 1700s, sea otters lived along the coast of the North Pacific Ocean, all the way from California to Alaska and over to Russia and Japan. In the mid-1700s, Russian explorers discovered that people would pay a lot of money for the thick pelts of sea otters. Word spread, and trading ships began to arrive off the coast of BC, looking for sea otter pelts. The First Nations people had always hunted small numbers of sea otters for their own use, but now they began to hunt more and more to trade for iron tools, blankets and guns. The sea otter pelts were shipped from BC to China, Russia and Europe, where they were sewn into coats, hats and blankets. The fur was so popular, and there was so much money to be made, that by the late 1920s every single sea otter off the coast of BC had been killed. Every single one.

But the story didn't end there. Fortunately, a few sea otters survived in other parts of the North Pacific Ocean.

TOP: Hauling a whale out of the water, Nanaimo.
IMAGE E-06683 COURTESY OF ROYAL BC MUSEUM, BC ARCHIVES

BOTTOM: A sea otter floats on its back, resting. JARED HOBBS

Today, the BC sea otter population is slowly returning because some concerned people took action to bring them back. In the late 1960s, eighty-nine sea otters were relocated from Alaska to the coast of BC. Many of the otters survived the move. Slowly but steadily, the population of sea otters in BC is growing. In 2008 over 4,500 sea otters were counted off the coast of BC. Sea otters are a good news story. More and more people are reporting seeing them swimming off the coast.

Sea otters play a special role in the coastal ecosystem. One of the animals that the otters eat are sea urchins, round creatures with hard shells and long purple or red spines. The urchins crawl along the rocks and eat kelp. When the sea otters were all hunted, the sea urchin population grew really large because it had no predators. With so many more sea urchins, there was much less kelp. Kelp creates what looks like a forest under the sea. Many fish and crabs live in kelp,

TOP: Sea urchins are covered in sharp spines. JENS WIETING

BOTTOM: Kelp forests provide habitat for crabs, fish, sea otters and many other marine species. THOMAS P. PESCHAK

MAP: Grizzly bears are no longer able to survive in many of the places they used to live.

OPPOSITE: Grizzly bear hair gets wet and matted in the rain, just like ours. IAN MCALLISTER

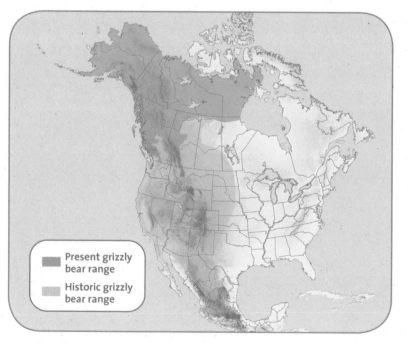

Present grizzly bear range

Historic grizzly bear range

and even whales will swim through kelp forests in search of food. Without kelp, all the species that depend on these underwater forests have to go elsewhere to find a home or find food, and not all will survive. With the return of the sea otters, the coastal ecosystem can come back into balance. The otters will eat the urchins, and there will be more kelp forests providing habitat for many other creatures.

Bears and Bear Rugs

Grizzly bears used to live throughout much of western North America. But over the years, as roads and cities and subdivisions expanded, grizzly bears have been displaced from 99 percent of their original habitat in the United States

ECO-STORY

A dream come true

When I was a young girl I had posters of sea otters on my bedroom wall. Something about them captured my imagination. They were cute, their alert eyes peering out from furry faces where they rested in the kelp beds. I knew they'd been hunted almost to **extinction**, that there were only a few in BC waters and that I might never see one in the wild. Looking at them on my wall, I felt a combination of sadness and hope.

When I started to spend time in the Great Bear Rainforest, I began hearing stories about sea otters. These days, the otters aren't so few and far between. In fact, when I confessed my lifelong dream of someday seeing a sea otter, people almost laughed at me! There are lots, I was told, along the outer coast. Finally, my moment came. I was on a small boat and there they were, their dark heads sticking out above the white water where the waves were crashing up against the rocky coastline. They weren't close, and the rough waves made it hard to see, but in that moment I knew what it was to have a dream come true. It was a reminder that things can change, that species can recover, and that I could let go of some of the concern for the otters that I'd been holding inside since I was a girl.

(not counting Alaska) and more than 60 percent of their original habitat in Canada.

To find all the food they need, these big bears require large areas of wilderness. Grizzly bears are losing their

VOICES FROM THE COAST

How things used to be
William Housty, Heiltsuk First Nation

Growing up in Bella Bella, William Housty was told many stories by his grandparents. When he was a teenager in the 1990s, he realized that the Heiltsuk people had their own origin myths. It was then that he started to really listen, and learn.

In the beginning it was hard. William wanted to stay home and listen to old stories, but his friends didn't think it was cool. But he had the support of his family and the community. Now many of his friends work with him and are involved in learning and reviving the Heiltsuk culture.

"Knowing the old stories has given me a lot more respect for the land and the people. Our people managed to live from the sea and the land. They were respectful and knew when they had taken enough. Respect also came because they knew the sea and the land could take your life if you weren't careful. In mythical times, animals could transform into humans and humans could turn into animals. Animals and humans took care of each other and lived among each other in harmony. We are missing this now.

"It's crazy to try and fathom how drastically things changed in the span of my grandfather's life. How things used to be sounds pretty amazing compared to what it is now. They used to smoke salmon by the thousands in the smokehouse. These days some rivers are lucky to get just a thousand salmon returning.

"When I learned about how things used to be, it brought to light that we have lost the connection to our land and sea. Now we have a store and don't have to go out and hunt and fish as much as we used to. Modern society has pulled people away from having a deep respect for the land and sea, and this has contributed to a loss of resources. If we had followed the balance in the old stories, would the salmon have gone the way they did?"

habitat as a result of roads, cities, logging and industrial developments. And the declining number of salmon is making it hard for them to gain enough weight to survive the winter hibernation. Grizzly bears also face trophy hunters, people who fly to BC from around the world to shoot bears and take their fur home as a trophy.

What would the Great Bear Rainforest be without bears? First Nations and environmentalists concerned about the bears have made sure that some habitat for grizzly bears has been protected and are campaigning to end the trophy hunt. For the bears to survive, there needs to be a ban on killing them for sport, more of their habitat needs to be protected and the salmon have to keep coming up the rivers each year.

Listening to the Stories

When we hear these stories about how the ocean has been changed and how the grizzly bears have lost so much of their habitat, it helps us understand how different the coast is now. It also helps us appreciate why the Great Bear Rainforest is so special and why so many people care about protecting it. We can make choices to protect the remaining salmon and the old forests the bears need. We can do this by protecting habitat and by choosing to take less from the world around us so that the plants and animals and fish can survive. But the first step, always, is to stop and listen to the stories.

TOP: Sockeye salmon swims upriver.
ANDREW S. WRIGHT

BOTTOM: Bull kelp is one of the fastest-growing seaweeds in the world.
ANDREW S. WRIGHT

"You may never know what results come of your actions. But if you do nothing, there will be no results."
—Mahatma Gandhi,
Indian independence leader
(1869–1948)

SCRATCH SCRATCH

CHAPTER SIX

Timber and Toilet Paper

First Nations have always harvested trees: for buildings, canoes, masks, artwork, tools and medicines. Historically, they felled trees by controlled burning or cut them down using tools with sharp stone or bone blades.

When the Europeans arrived, larger-scale logging began along the south coast of BC. At first, many settlers saw the trees as a nuisance, something they needed to get rid of so that they could grow food crops and build settlements. Later they realized they could make money by selling the timber. Without asking the First Nations who lived there, the provincial government began encouraging settlers and logging companies to cut the big coastal trees. It seemed at first that the trees were so big and there were so many that they would never run out.

At that time, cutting even just one tree took a lot of time and effort. Two loggers worked together on each tree.

"Don't be afraid to question authority. Authority should be earned, not appointed. The 'experts' are often proven wrong (they used to believe that the earth was flat!). You don't have to be an expert to have a valuable opinion or to speak out on an issue."

—Angela Bischoff and **Tooker Gomberg,** environmental activists (from "Ten Commandments for Changing the World," 1996, www.greenspiration.org)

OPPOSITE: Standing in a recent clear-cut. This stump is 3.4 meters (11 feet) across and 10.7 meters (35 feet) in circumference. TJ WATT

One on each end of a long handsaw, they sawed back and forth, slowly cutting through the tree.

Once a tree came down, it had to be removed from the forest. Some of the trees were so big the loggers used dynamite to split them into smaller pieces that could be moved. Trees were hauled out of the forest using oxen and horses, and later, machinery, trains and trucks.

As technology has changed, the speed of logging has increased. By the 1930s, chainsaws had made it possible for one person to cut down a tree. Later, giant machines called feller bunchers moved through the forest, plucking trees off at their base, cutting off the branches, and stacking them in a big pile, all in a matter of minutes. This **mechanization** has made it possible to cut trees down faster than ever before. At the same time, it has meant that there are fewer jobs available for people who want to work in the woods.

TOP: The early days of logging, Cowichan Lake, BC.
IMAGE C-05301 COURTESY OF ROYAL BC MUSEUM, BC ARCHIVES

BOTTOM: Piling logs onto a truck for transport to a mill.
TJ WATT

RIGHT: Mist rises over the rainforest.
ANDREW S. WRIGHT

OPPOSITE: A giant western red cedar in the Bella Coola Valley.
CRISTINA MITTERMEIER / iLCP

After a tree is cut, it is piled onto a large truck with other logs and taken to a mill, where it is turned into lumber or paper. Really good-quality wood might be used for making furniture or musical instruments. In the early days of BC logging, the wood was used to build the towns of Vancouver and Victoria. It was exported by boat as far as England and Australia to be used in shipbuilding. Wood from BC was used to build the railways and was shipped to the prairies to be used in building homesteads.

The Last of the Rainforest Giants

Early settlers thought the old-growth forests would go on forever. But they were wrong. We have all the equipment we need to cut trees down quickly, but there are fewer trees

ECO-STORY

A city in the forest

Growing up in Vancouver, I was surrounded by pavement and buildings, as well as chestnut and cherry trees that had been brought and planted to remind immigrants of their former homes. There are very few cedar trees or Douglas-firs growing anywhere along the streets of Vancouver. I remember being shocked when I saw pictures that showed the logging—from only a hundred years earlier—in the very part of the city where I lived. The trees were so big they made the men who were cutting them down look tiny. I realized that this city I lived in was once a forest, with wildlife and salmon streams.

We need places to live, obviously, and I really liked my city. To me, seeing these old pictures was a reminder that if we can build cities with a smaller footprint (more people in a smaller area), then more of the forests in the outlying areas can remain standing.

This big tree was cut down by hand, Vancouver, 1890.
IMAGE A-04893 COURTESY OF ROYAL BC MUSEUM, BC ARCHIVES

left to cut. There are not many un-logged valleys left on the entire coast of BC. All but 1.2 percent of the old-growth Douglas-fir forests on Vancouver Island have been logged. On the mainland coast, logging has slowly but surely spread northward.

Why is this cause for concern? The big trees took many hundreds of years to grow. Once they are cut down, we won't see trees like this again in our lifetime. Birds and wildlife that depend on old-growth forests can't survive in a clear-cut or a young forest. Salmon can't survive in a clear-cut. Without the shade provided by the trees, the water becomes too warm for young salmon. Also, the roots of trees hold soil in place. When a forest is logged, rain causes the soil to slide down hillsides and into streams, where it can bury the gravel that salmon need

VOICES FROM THE COAST

A young forestry worker
Chief Earl Maquinna George

Chief Earl Maquinna George grew up in the village of Ahousaht, on the west coast of Vancouver Island. When he was just twelve years old, in 1938, his family traveled by boat to Rivers Inlet to find work in what is now the Great Bear Rainforest. His father and brother went fishing, while Earl worked in a cannery. After a long summer of hard work and seventeen-hour days, he had made $13.00. When he was sixteen years old, Earl started working for a logging company.

"I was put on the nightshift, piling the heavy timbers as they came out from the mill. I learned how to operate and maneuver them by using a levering tool called a peevee. I was a youngster, and the work was heavy, the hours were long and the noise was terrible. Throughout the night I could hear the saws screaming in my ears, but I had to make a living."

(From *Living on the Edge: Nuu-Chah-Nulth History from an Ahousaht Chief's Perspective*)

for spawning. Without forests to slow the water, flooding becomes a more frequent problem for anyone who lives near a river.

Ancient trees are important for the health of forest ecosystems. But there is something else about them, something that goes beyond science. Standing next to an ancient tree is a humbling experience. To touch its bark and think that this tree has been alive for over a thousand years, that this very tree was hundreds of years old already when Europeans stumbled upon the shores of North America, was ancient when Canada was formed as a country, and is still standing today… History, and our place on this Earth, are put into perspective in the presence of very old trees.

For these reasons and more, many people want all clear-cutting of old-growth forests to stop. They are concerned about the environmental impact of logging and are worried that soon there won't be any big trees left. These people have made their voices heard with demonstrations, letter writing, blockades and **markets campaigns**. As a result, in some places logging has slowed, is now done differently or has stopped entirely. But in other parts of the coast, the big old trees continue to be cut down.

Logging companies now cut the smaller second-growth trees on the south coast and operate farther up the coast, where they find the remaining big old trees. Much of the wood is exported to the United States, Japan, Europe and, increasingly, China. Forestry jobs used to support many families and communities in BC,

OPPOSITE: Road blockade to stop logging in the Great Bear Rainforest. GREENPEACE/GREG KING

DID YOU KNOW

How paper is made from trees

After a tree is cut down in a forest, its branches are removed and it becomes a round log. It is taken by truck to a sawmill, where it is cut on all four sides to make it square. The square log is then cut into smaller planks. As the log is cut, the bark, bits of wood and sawdust are left behind. This leftover material is then sent to a pulp mill to be made into paper. Or sometimes trees are sent straight from the forest to pulp mills.

In a pulp mill, the wood chips are broken down, using a combination of steam and chemicals, until they become a sticky paste, kind of like porridge. This paste is called pulp. Used paper can also be put into the process at this point and recycled into pulp. The pulp is then drained on a screen and pressed to get the water out. Once dried, it can be cut into sheets. This is how we make cardboard boxes, brown paper bags, newsprint for newspapers, writing paper and even toilet paper.

Pulp mill. MIKE AMBACH

TAKE ACTION

Recycle as little as possible!

You've probably heard of the famous three Rs: Reduce, Reuse, Recycle. Many of us are pretty good at the recycling part. Of course we need to keep recycling, but it's important not to forget the first two Rs—reducing and reusing. Not everything can be recycled. Also, the process of recycling requires lots of energy to make new things out of the old ones and often uses new raw materials from the earth. Reducing and reusing are actually the most important actions you can take to reduce your **ecological footprint** on this planet.

Reducing simply means buying and acquiring less stuff: thinking about whether or not you really need a new iPod or cell phone or pair of jeans or plastic bag at the grocery store. Reusing means using what you already have for as long as possible and then finding a creative new use for it when it wears out rather than just throwing it away. Patch up the holes in your old clothes, or cut them up and sew them into new outfits; fix your electronic gadgets rather than just buying new ones; lend a book to a friend so they don't need to buy one; hold a clothing swap to exchange clothes with your friends (what is old and boring to you will be new to someone else). When you or your friends and family have absolutely no use for something, that's the time to recycle it if you can.

even though BC forestry has never maximized the number of jobs that could be created. Many trees are turned into basic lumber, a process which doesn't require very many workers, or are exported as raw logs. In comparison, making the choice to turn a tree into high-value products, such as flooring, window frames, furniture or musical instruments, would make it possible to employ more people for every tree cut down. But these days, the availability of fewer high-value trees, combined with the choice to mechanize harvesting and not process the wood in BC, has meant that forestry-related jobs have become few and far between.

Ecosystems and Our Economy

Political decisions and management decisions about how much of any given species can be harvested are often based on the amount of money there is to be made. Profit leads

Unloading crab traps. CRISTINA MITTERMEIER / iLCP

to economic growth, which is the goal of many politicians and business leaders. But the problem with seeking continuous economic growth is that our economy is not separate from our environment. Everything in our economy (food, toys, computers, bicycles, clothes, etc.) comes from our environment. We extract resources from the world around us, consume them as products we eat or use, and then dump the waste back into the Earth. Our Earth is a **finite** ecosystem, which means there is only so much that we can take from the natural world to feed our economy, and only so much waste that the Earth can absorb, before natural processes stop functioning properly. The constant effort to extract more and more resources is actually an ecological impossibility over the long term. Our survival depends on learning to live within the limits of ecosystems.

In the case of ancient trees, they have financial value. But they also have ecological value, and they are valued culturally by coastal First Nations. If these other values are taken into consideration when management decisions are made, we will be more likely to have healthy forests in the future.

On the Blockade

Sometimes it takes more direct action to make your voice heard. Maybe you have met with politicians, written letters to the editor, held public gatherings on an issue or negotiated with companies, but your voice still isn't being heard. If the laws

DID YOU KNOW

Where does stuff come from?

Where does all the stuff in your life come from? It's not always easy to find out, but asking questions and being curious is a good beginning. Tracking where and how things are made, and what they are made with, will show you the ways that each item we use is connected to—and comes from—ecosystems around the world.

The wood in our houses and the paper in our books come from forests that are habitat to birds and wildlife. Our pets eat seafood, caught somewhere in the world's oceans, that may have been food for larger fish. Our bicycles are made with metals that are mined from the earth. Mining can sometimes contaminate water and damage fish habitat. When you dig into the details of where stuff comes from, you find that everything in our lives comes from the natural world. That doesn't mean we should stop eating or riding our bikes or talking on the phone. But when we understand where things really come from and what happened to the ecosystems they were taken from, we might decide to make careful choices about how much stuff we really need.

And where does it go when we are done with it? Nothing disappears. It all gets put somewhere. Watch Annie Leonard's "The Story of Stuff" at www.storyofstuff.com to learn more.

TAKE ACTION

Contact your politicians

If you are concerned about something, such as how many trees are being cut down where you live, one simple action you can take is to contact your politicians. Governments, at least democratic ones, are supposed to care what their citizens think. If you phone them, write to them or meet with them, they should listen. Politicians may not do exactly what you want, but the more people who speak up, the more likely they are to listen. One handwritten letter is assumed to represent hundreds of people who share the same views. Emailing or phoning and leaving a message about something you are concerned about only takes a moment. Governments should listen to everyone's point of view. So it is important that you add your voice to the mix! Tell them your concerns.

haven't changed and the proposed activity hasn't been stopped, **nonviolent direct action** is sometimes used as a last resort.

Nonviolent direct action is when people confront, disrupt or actively oppose—without using violence—laws or activities they perceive to be harmful or unjust. For example, people may occupy a workplace or disrupt activities such as logging or mining in order to encourage governments and corporations to behave in more socially just and/or environmentally sustainable ways. It can sometimes involve getting arrested. Nonviolent direct action has been used around the world in countless important moments in history, such as the civil rights movement in the United States.

In Clayoquot Sound, on the west coast of Vancouver Island, environmentalists decided to block a logging road after all other tactics had failed to stop clear-cut logging. Over twelve thousand people participated in the blockade

over the summer of 1993—the largest protest in Canadian history. Each day, the police asked the protestors to clear the road. Those who had decided to risk arrest stayed seated and had to be carried off one by one. Over nine hundred people, from age ten to eighty-one, were arrested that summer. *For more on this story, see Take Action! on page 74.*

OPPOSITE (TOP): Women's Day protest march, Clayoquot Sound, 1993.
CHIP VINAI

OPPOSITE (BOTTOM): Risking arrest to stop logging in Clayoquot Sound, 1993.
SARAH TURNER

ECO-STORY

Dwarfed by giants

When I get near an ancient tree, or even a tree that is just a few hundred years old, I crane my neck to look up into its high branches. But more than anything else, I feel an urge to get close to it and, if possible, climb onto it, even just onto an exposed root. Resting my forehead on the trunk of the tree, I can smell the dusty bark and the sweet sap. The most alive part of a tree is just under the bark, where it transports water and sugars and minerals up and down between the roots and the branches. Touching the bark (watch out for sticky sap!), it is almost possible to sense the energy flow beneath my hands. And it is amazing to think that I am in the presence of something that has been alive, in this very spot, for hundreds of years before I was born.

One thing I really like about standing under an ancient tree is how small it makes me feel. So much of our lives—our economy and the industrial resource extraction that provides our food, fish and wood products—is based on an assumption that we can control nature, that we are somehow greater than nature and can make it serve our purposes. When I stand on a wide-open mountaintop, look out over the ocean or stand under a big tree, I am reminded that we are all just small pieces of a bigger puzzle. This gives me comfort, and hope. Comfort because I am reminded of the strength and resiliency of the natural world. These ancient trees have lived through a lot, and no matter how badly we screw up, life will go on. And the trees give me hope because they have the power to remind us of our place in the natural world.

TJ WATT

TAKE ACTION

Do what feels right

Marguerite Drescher was twelve years old when she and her parents and younger brother took the train from Nova Scotia to support the protests in Clayoquot Sound. By the time the train reached the west coast, she had decided to sit on the road and be arrested.

"I loved the feeling of being an activist. Reading about the rainforest, singing at the protests and feeling a deep emotional connection for the Earth. I had crushes on the teens on the train and longed to be a little older. As we neared BC, I started to think about the road blockades we would be attending. I listened to stories about Greenpeace and people in trees, arrests and injustice. I felt passionate and thrilled by the idea of being a part of something so big and powerful. I told my parents about wanting to sit on the road when we got there. They were not nuts about the idea. I was sure though, and they allowed me to make my own decision.

"The day of the blockade was possibly one of the most intense days of my life. It was frightening and exhilarating. I was terrified to the point of tears, sitting on the road at four AM in the dark with the other protesters. There were cameras and reporters, megaphones and huge logging trucks, singing and signs, banners and shouting. I cried through the news interviews, where I was repeatedly asked ▶▶

Continued on page 75

All But Gone, But We Have a Choice

When we learn about how things used to be, and then when we witness the poor health of ecosystems today, it is a natural response to get worried. One billion people in the world rely entirely on seafood as a source of protein. If there are no longer any fish to catch, how will we survive? How does it feel to know that some animals are so rare that we may never see them? Where will the grizzly bears and the marbled murrelets and the tailed frogs live if the old-growth forests are all gone? And how can families continue to live on the coast if there are no fishing or forestry jobs?

So much has been harvested from the ocean and the forest that some species, like the right whales and the marbled murrelets, are all but gone. We are all connected in a web of life, so when one species becomes extinct or endangered, many other species are affected. As plants and animals become less abundant, fewer options remain for people who live on the coast to find food or to make a living.

Some of these stories are hard to hear. When you realize how much has already been lost, it can be upsetting.

Getting upset, sad or angry is a normal reaction. Choosing to not think about it and pretending everything is fine is also a common reaction to problems that seem too big. But now that you've heard these stories, you can choose to make a difference in your world. Lots of people, young and old, have done just that.

Trees and animals don't just disappear. Sometimes, as we have seen with the abalone or the right whales, where there is money to be made, animals are harvested to the point of extinction. Or sometimes, as is the case with the eulachon, not enough value is placed on them and decisions are made that reduce the chances of their survival. And sometimes we can see the impact of our actions and decide to change what we are doing before it is too late.

For example, instead of accepting that there were no longer any sea otters off the coast of BC, a few people decided to do what they could to bring the otters back. We can all make similar choices—small or large. It can be as simple (and as complicated) as drinking tap water out of a reusable water bottle or joining a protest march. We can accept the loss of the abalone and the eulachon, we can stand back and watch the decline of the bears and the salmon and the ancient trees, or we can choose to try and bring them back. We can choose what future we want for the coast depending on what actions we take in our own lives. Remember, we are all characters in the Earth's story, and we can change the ending. The choice is yours; you have a say in what happens next.

As storyteller Thomas King writes in *The Truth about Stories*, this story is now yours. "Do with it what you will. Cry over it. Get angry. Forget it. But don't say in the years to come that you would have lived your life differently if only you had heard this story. You've heard it now."

TAKE ACTION

▶▶ *Continued from page 74*

how old I was and where my parents were. I told them that I wanted to be there and my parents chose not to. I felt fortunate to do what I thought was right. I was arrested with two other minors and taken back to the police station as the sun came up. We were released to our guardians with a warning to stay out of trouble. I was angry that we were not taken more seriously."

In fact, Marguerite and the hundreds of other people arrested did make a difference. As a result of the protest, parts of Clayoquot Sound were made off-limits to logging. In the rest of the area, the logging would be more sustainable and would follow the recommendations of a panel of scientists, and the BC government committed to talking with communities across the province about land use in the hopes of avoiding more conflicts of this type.

OPPOSITE: Rally to end old-growth logging. TJ WATT

"It's much rarer for a kid to oppose a development than an adult. I think people might tend to listen more to a kid."
—Andrew Holleman (12), environmental activist (from *It's Our World, Too!* by Phillip Hoose).

CHAPTER SEVEN

Salmon: A story of mystery, barbecues, food coloring and hope

Salmon, Food for Us All

Canned salmon, smoked salmon, barbecued salmon, baked salmon, candied salmon…Salmon cooked over a fire, salmon steaks, lox on a bagel, salmon patties, salmon served on a cedar plank, salmon served in a big house…

And that's just for us humans. There is also salmon for the wolves, salmon for the bears, salmon for the eagles, salmon for the ravens, salmon for the trees. Salmon are food for so many creatures and are a key component in a healthy coastal temperate rainforest. Salmon are important to coastal First Nations as a major source of food, but also as a part of their culture. There are salmon songs and salmon dances and salmon masks, and there are salmon carved on totem poles.

Do you eat salmon? What is your favorite way to eat it? Do you know where in the ocean your salmon comes from?

"Never doubt that a small group of thoughtful, committed citizens can change the world; indeed, it's the only thing that ever has."
—Margaret Mead, American anthropologist (1901–1978)

OPPOSITE: An eagle snatches a fish out of the water.
DOUGLAS NEASLOSS

DID YOU KNOW

Shellfish aquaculture

Aquaculture, the word for fish and shellfish farming, can be an important source of food. Farming shellfish is very different from farming salmon. Salmon farms are environmentally intensive operations that require the input of all kinds of food, chemicals and antibiotics. Because salmon are **carnivores**, raising them (in the ocean or in pens on land) requires large numbers of fish to be caught elsewhere and used to feed them. Shellfish, on the other hand, get all their food simply by filtering the water that passes by. Oysters, mussels and scallops are all **filter feeders** and can be easily farmed. Shellfish aquaculture can provide sustainable sources of seafood.

ABOVE: With a belly full of salmon, a grizzly bear takes a nap. ANDREW S. WRIGHT

OPPOSITE (TOP): Cooking salmon over a fire. QQS (EYES) PROJECTS SOCIETY

OPPOSITE (BOTTOM): A salmon farm. Each net holds thousands (often hundreds of thousands) of salmon. ANDREW S. WRIGHT

Is it Pacific salmon or Atlantic salmon? Is it wild or is it farmed? Can you taste the difference?

Not All Salmon Are the Same

Atlantic salmon spawn in Europe and along the east coast of North America. There is only one type of Atlantic salmon. In comparison, there are five types of Pacific salmon that spawn along the west coast of North America, and there are other types of Pacific salmon that spawn in Asia. Here in North America, the five major species of Pacific salmon are the Chinook, coho, pink, chum and sockeye. Each type of salmon is different: in size, shape, the number of years they spend in the ocean before returning to the rivers to spawn, the time of year they return and which part of the river systems they use for spawning. For much of the year there are salmon spawning, somewhere, in the forests along the west coast.

Chinook are the largest and are nicknamed "king" salmon; coho are good jumpers; male pinks grow a big hump on their back when spawning and are also called "humpbacks"; chum are sometimes called "dog" salmon; and sockeye have the reddest—and some say tastiest—flesh. Chinook spawn in large rivers, coho spawn in the small streams that flow into large rivers, pinks spawn in estuaries, and chum spawn in small channels near estuaries. Sockeye spawn either in lakes or streams that flow into lakes, because juvenile sockeye are unique in that they must spend a year or more in a freshwater lake before heading out to the ocean.

Salmon on the Menu

Some years, the bears in the Great Bear Rainforest can't find enough salmon to eat. The hungry bears look skinny, with their ribs sticking out.

At the same time, salmon is for sale in stores and restaurants all over North America. How is this possible, if there are so few wild salmon left? Well, if the salmon on the menu is wild salmon, then we are eating the salmon that would have gone to feed the bears and the wolves and the coastal communities. And much of the time the salmon on the menu is farmed fish.

All About Fish Farms

If you choose to eat salmon but are concerned that there are so few wild salmon left, is it a better option to eat salmon that was grown at a fish farm? Salmon farms provide an important source of food, and they provide jobs to coastal communities. But the communities on BC's north coast

ECO-STORY

Salmon eagles

Bald eagles are graceful birds, and it's not until you see one up close that you realize how huge they are. The wingspan of an eagle can be as much as 2.4 meters (8 feet)! Bald eagles eat so many salmon that they have been nicknamed the "salmon eagles." With their powerful eyesight, they can spot a fish from high above. I've seen eagles swoop down out of the sky, grab a fish out of the water with their talons and fly off. But sometimes, if the fish is too heavy, the eagle won't be able to fly with it. Instead, the bird will swim to shore, tugging the fish in its talons and using its wings as paddles.

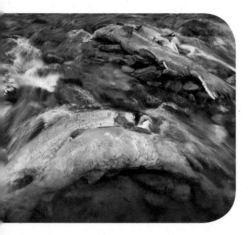

After spawning, salmon die, and the cycle of life continues.
ANDREW S. WRIGHT

don't want fish farms in the ocean. They don't think the environmental impact is worth the risk. Thousands of people (including First Nations, conservationists, commercial fishermen, sport fishers and local municipalities) came together to protect wild salmon by demanding that fish farms be kept out of their region. The BC government listened and, in 2008, declared a moratorium on fish farms on the north coast.

But there are still fish farms on the central and south coast of BC. People on the coast talk about how you can tell a farmed fish by how the meat falls apart, and they say it is easy to taste the difference. When you eat a farmed fish, you are eating red food coloring (used to make the Atlantic salmon look like Pacific salmon), antibiotics (used to treat disease) and chemicals (used to kill pests). And you are eating all the little fish that were caught

VOICES FROM THE COAST

Greeting the salmon
Helen Clifton, Gitga'at First Nation

Helen, a grandmother and respected elder of the Gitga'at First Nation, lives in Hartley Bay.

"It's not just us that depend on the salmon; it's the whole ecosystem, whether you're a four-legged or a swimmer or a two-legged like us. Before the rains come, the salmon school up at the mouth of the river. We watch them flipping and jumping into the air, so silvery. The bears are waiting for the same salmon that we are waiting for. And while we wait, we are eating the same berries that the bears are eating, the wild currants and the highbush cranberries.

"When it starts raining and the creeks fill up with water, the salmon come upstream. Our people would call out a greeting to the salmon. I don't think we could exist without the salmon." PHOTO OF HELEN CLIFTON BY CRISTINA MITTERMEIER / iLCP

to feed the salmon: it takes 1.4 to 2.3 kilograms (3 to 5 pounds) of fish from elsewhere in the world to produce one pound of farmed fish. This is not sustainable for the world's oceans. The big open nets that the salmon are raised in allow disease, pesticides, fish food, sewage and escaped fish to move between the farm and the rest of the ocean. Fish farms on land—imagine a huge swimming pool—wouldn't have as many of these environmental impacts. Some people see these as a good alternative.

Where Have All the Wild Salmon Gone?

If you are lucky enough to visit a salmon stream when the salmon are spawning, you will know it! They are easy to spot, resting in the pools of water and jumping up over waterfalls. You can hear them thrashing around in the shallow water, moving upriver or using their tails to dig a good place to spawn. And you can smell the stink of rotting flesh all along the banks of the river.

TAKE ACTION

Know your fish

Many people eat farmed salmon without knowing where it comes from. There are no rules saying that farmed fish needs to be labeled as such. Wild salmon, however, is often labeled. Generally, if the label doesn't say *wild*, you can probably assume it's from a fish farm.

Now that you know some of the health and environmental concerns, you can make up your own mind about whether you want to eat farmed salmon or not. Talk to the people in your family who do the grocery shopping—let them know what you think and ask them to make careful choices in the grocery store. If money is a factor and wild salmon is too expensive, perhaps there is some other fish caught near where you live that is more affordable. Or maybe you don't want to eat fish at all.

A spirit bear looks for food at the edge of the ocean.
DOUGLAS NEASLOSS

"Be the change you want to see in the world."
—Mahatma Gandhi,
Indian independence leader
(1869–1948)

VOICES FROM THE COAST

Salmon Are Sacred

Molina Dawson (15), Dzawada'enuxw First Nation

"I, for one, am not going to just sit around and watch while our indigenous wildlife slowly gets picked off, only to be replaced by a bunch of freaky farm fish!"

Molina, also known as Ogwila'ogwa, from the Dzawada'enuxw First Nation in Kingcome Inlet, was fourteen years old when she joined the Salmon Are Sacred "Get Out Migration" in 2010—a walk to raise awareness about the impact of fish farms on wild salmon. She was one of about thirty people who walked the entire route: sixteen days and over 400 kilometers (249 miles), all the way from Port McNeill on northern Vancouver Island to Victoria. At each town they passed they were joined by more walkers. On the last day, thousands of people filled the streets of Victoria for a big rally.

Molina said she joined the walk because salmon are important to her community in Kingcome Inlet, because she understands the impact the fish farms are having on wild salmon and because she wants to try and keep what's left of her home safe. "It's my home and I don't want to lose it," she said. "The salmon are a part of us." Molina's commitment was an inspiration to others. Her uncle walked with her the entire way, and her dad drove one of the support vehicles. "They came because I came," she said. She said that her motivation to keep walking came from the support she knew she had back home. The night before she left, her community held a potluck dinner to send her off.

Molina said all those days of walking were "amazing." She felt it was important because it gave people who were already concerned something to get involved in. They could join the walk or organize events in their community. And it got more people aware of the issues facing wild salmon.

Molina thinks that young people can see things more clearly than adults and so are often in a better position to help out. "Everyone's in a position to do something," she said. "You've just got to find what it is." PHOTO OF MOLINA DAWSON BY KATE BRAUER

Wearing regalia to honor wild salmon.
MARK WORTHING

In 2010, sockeye salmon returned to the Fraser River in numbers not seen in almost a hundred years. There was work in fishing, sockeye was for sale on docks, and people flocked to see the red spawning salmon. It was a celebration of salmon. Scientists didn't understand why there were so many more than expected. It seemed that the salmon were giving us another chance. They *can* come back.

But when you look more closely, all is not well for salmon in BC. Not even for the Fraser River sockeye. While 2010 was an amazing year for some smaller rivers that flow into the Fraser, that very same year some other streams entering the Fraser saw so few returning salmon they were listed as endangered. In 2009, fewer sockeye swam up the Fraser River than ever before—so few that a government inquiry was launched into why the numbers of fish had declined so drastically. Because the life cycle for sockeye is four years, the offspring from the sockeye spawning in 2010 won't return to the rivers until 2014. How many fish return in the years in between will be a different story.

Up the coast in the Great Bear Rainforest, the rivers are quiet these days—quieter than normal. Some rivers have hardly any fish. And it's not just the salmon that are missing. The birds that normally hop around in search of salmon eggs aren't there. Bears come to a river, look over on one side for salmon, then the other, then turn and walk back into the woods. There are no wolf tracks in the mud. It is an eerie silence.

Why aren't the salmon coming back to the rivers to spawn? We don't know all the reasons, but we know many of them. One simple reason is that we have caught too many. Another reason is that logging or road building near a salmon stream can change the temperature and the acidity of the water, which makes it hard for the salmon

TAKE ACTION

Choose your seafood carefully
You can make a difference by choosing what you eat. The SeaChoice cards (www.seachoice.org) tell you which types of seafood are harvested sustainably, and which are best avoided.

Dead and decaying salmon provide nutrients to the river. JENS WIETING

Celebrating salmon with creative art.
JENS WIETING

to survive. The young salmon that travel past fish farms on their way to the sea sometimes die from the diseases and parasites, such as sea lice, that they catch from the captive fish. Out in the ocean, pollution and changing conditions due to **global warming** are affecting the survival of salmon. And we are "fishing down the food chain." That means that because we have already caught many of the big fish, we are now fishing for smaller and smaller types of fish. Salmon are carnivores—they eat smaller fish. So if we are catching these smaller fish, we are making it harder for the salmon to find the food they need.

For all these reasons, and probably more, the salmon aren't returning to spawn in the numbers that they used to. For those who remember how the rivers used to be filled with salmon, parts of the coast today feel like ghost lands. Something is missing. The rivers are quiet, freezers are not full of fish, and the wild creatures are hungry.

Learning from the Past

Atlantic cod used to live in large numbers off the coast of Newfoundland. Ever since Europeans arrived in Canada, cod were caught and shipped off to Europe. Fish stocks in the waters around Europe were already low, due to heavy fishing, so people in Europe were eager for fish from Canada. Over the years, the use of technology allowed more cod to be found and caught each year.

Scientists kept warning that the cod populations couldn't last. The people who lived in coastal communities sounded the alarm about overfishing. But the cod fishery continued unchecked, despite all the warnings. Why? Because the fishing business created jobs, and there was money to be made.

In 1991 the government reduced the number of fish that could be caught but it was too late. By 1992 there were so few cod left that the federal government had to completely shut down the fishery, just as was predicted by all those people for all those years. With no fish, the jobs were gone. Making money had been a higher priority than maintaining the health of ocean ecosystems. No one listened to the people who saw this coming, and now the fish are gone. Twenty years later, the cod still haven't returned in numbers that would support a fishery. Is this the future for the Pacific salmon?

Why Does It Matter to Me If There Are Salmon or Not?

Even people who don't live in the Great Bear Rainforest are deeply connected to what happens there. Some connections are easy to see. If we like to eat salmon (wild or farmed), we are partially responsible for their decline. Other connections are harder to see. The wood in our houses may come from forests that, when logged, altered salmon spawning habitat. And we are all part of one global ecosystem. It matters to the survival of all of us that there are intact forests producing the oxygen that we breathe and helping to slow climate change. These forests depend on the health of the salmon.

Finally, all of this matters because you can make a difference! You can choose a better ending to this story. Just as we all play a role in the decline of the salmon, so too are we

TAKE ACTION

Streamkeepers

Streamkeepers are people of all ages who are helping to protect, restore and monitor salmon habitat. Looking after the streams where you live, and making them livable for salmon, is a great way to take responsibility for your own backyard. Streamkeepers plant native trees and shrubs along a stream to provide shade and food for the young salmon, and they remove garbage and other debris from streams. Sometimes streamkeepers carefully place large boulders or logs in the stream to slow down the water, create gravel beds for spawning and offer hiding places for the fish.

Painting salmon on storm drains.
ZOANN MORTEN

If we do not change our direction, we are likely to end up where we are headed.
—**Chinese proverb**

Standing up for wild salmon

Alexandra Morton

In 1984, marine biologist Alexandra Morton moved to the Broughton Archipelago, a group of islands located off the northeastern corner of Vancouver Island, to study and film killer whales. Why are the whales cruising along with their dorsal fins out of the water like sharks? she wondered. The fishermen knew. It's because the spring salmon are just below the glacial meltwater at the top of the ocean; if the whales swim along at that level, the salmon are easy prey. Why do the whales come back to the same bay at the same time each year? The fishermen said the whales arrive when the salmon are gathering to go upriver.

When fish farms were established near where Alexandra lives, at first she welcomed them, thinking they would bring new families to her small community. But over time, the fish farms mechanized and employed fewer and fewer people. When the farms installed noise devices underwater in order to scare off the seals that preyed on the fish, the sound was deafening to the whales. Killer whales need to be able to hear in order to "see" underwater and to communicate with one another. The noise devices are as loud as a jet at takeoff. The resident whales promptly left the area and never came back.

Over the years, Alexandra has witnessed the impact of the fish farms on salmon and other marine life. She has written thousands of pages of letters to government to express her concerns. At first, nobody listened to her. So she began to work with other scientists to research the environmental impacts of the fish farms on wild species. Even with the scientific evidence, the government still did not appear to be listening. So in 2010 Alexandra took to the streets, mobilizing the Salmon Are Sacred "Get Out Migration," which saw thousands of people demanding the closure of open net-cage fish farms. "This is a test," she said. "Do we live in a democracy?"

With so many citizens from all walks of life demanding that fish farms be moved out of the ocean, will the government listen to the people who live on the coast or will it continue to prioritize the interests of the foreign corporations that own the fish farms?

The verdict is still unknown. But it is clear that by speaking up for wild salmon, Alexandra has helped inspire a growing movement of people who want a future with wild salmon in it.

Taking to the streets to speak up for wild salmon. CAITLYN VERNON

connected to the possible solutions. No matter where you live, you can play an important role in bringing back the wild salmon.

Salmon for the Future

If you visualize the future for salmon on the coast, what does it look like? Are there wild salmon? Are there enough for us to eat without worrying about whether we are impacting their future? Are there people with fishing jobs? Are the bears still hungry?

Visualizing the future you want to see is a useful way to figure out what choices you need to make today. It's called **backcasting**. First you imagine the world you want to see. Then you figure out what steps are needed in order to create this world.

Sometimes the day-to-day realities make it hard to imagine that the world could be different. But all through history, major changes have come about because people dare to dream about, and work toward, things that at first seem impossible. Imagine what you want to see happen, and start taking the necessary steps toward that dream. The Spanish poet Antonio Machado (1875–1939) said, "The road is created as we walk it together." This means that as we start taking steps toward our goals, achieving those goals becomes more and more possible.

What Future Do You Want to Live In?

The future of salmon is uncertain along the coast of BC. We could keep on eating lots of salmon and not do anything to protect their spawning habitat, and the numbers of salmon might continue to decline. Or we could eat less and

TAKE ACTION

Bringing salmon back to cities

If you live west of the Rocky Mountains, between California and Alaska, even if you live in a city, it's possible that there used to be salmon where you live. Restoring salmon habitat is not just about protecting or restoring forests in rural areas. It is also about supporting the return of salmon to urban streams. In cities, most streams have been buried underground, in culverts and storm sewers. Some communities have "daylighted" these streams. This means that they have opened up the urban streams to the light of day, where people can see them and trees can be planted alongside the water. With proper spawning habitat, the salmon can come back.

Vancouver's Old Streams

Vancouver's streams once had salmon in them. Today the streams are still there, but most are underground.

UBC LIBRARY 2011, FROM *Vancouver's Old Streams* BY SHARON J. PROCTOR, VANCOUVER PUBLIC AQUARIUM ASSOCIATION, 1978

TAKE ACTION

Youth in action

Twelve-year-old Andrew Holleman successfully stopped the development of condominiums in a forest he loved, near his home in Massachusetts. He saved the forest and the endangered species that live there by researching the species and the laws that protect them, talking to everyone in his neighborhood, starting a petition, writing letters to newspaper editors and giving speeches at town hearings.

"It's been said that we don't inherit our land from our parents—we borrow it from our children. That's the attitude you have to take. You're a child; it's your land. You're gonna be around a lot longer than these adults; you have more reason to care. Why not fight for it? They'll ruin your chance if they screw up your future. It's our earth. I challenge kids to protect it. If we don't do it, no one else is going to."

(From *It's Our World, Too!* by Phillip Hoose)

protect their habitat, but their numbers could still decline due to fish farms or changes in the ocean resulting from climate change. It's complicated. Any single action we take does not automatically guarantee a certain future for the salmon. But every action has consequences and will lead us either in the direction of a future without salmon or a future with salmon.

As we saw with the Fraser River sockeye in 2010, the salmon are resilient. We can choose a future with fish in the rivers, where the wolves are well fed. In this future, the First Nations people have all the food they need, and there are jobs for people who want to work in fishing. The bears are so full of salmon that their bellies drag along the ground and they flop down on rocks in the middle of the river to sleep, too full to do anything else. The trees can grow big and strong again, fortified with marine fertilizer from the salmon. And people who don't live on the coast can eat salmon also, but maybe not quite as

Sockeye salmon head upriver to spawn. ANDREW S. WRIGHT

often as before. Salmon have shown us that they can come back. This future is possible.

How can we get there? It might mean that nobody eats any wild salmon at all for a few years, so they can come back each year in greater numbers. It might mean that the food needs of the people who live on the coast are prioritized, so that even if fewer fish are caught, the First Nations still have food. It might mean setting aside protected areas in the ocean where no fishing is allowed. It might mean making different decisions about how fishing is done and where it is done. It might mean making sure that fish farms are not located in places where juvenile salmon pass by. It might mean protecting more spawning habitat upriver by protecting old-growth forests. It might mean that where logging has already happened, spawning habitat is restored by planting trees along the banks of streams. All of these things are entirely possible. If enough of us make the choice to save the wild salmon, we can do it.

TOP: Resident killer whales eat only salmon and prefer some kinds of salmon more than others. MILES RITTER

BOTTOM: A fish gets interviewed. MARK WORTHING

All the flowers of all the tomorrows are in the seeds of today.
—Indian proverb

CHAPTER EIGHT

Saving the Trees

The future is unknown for BC's wild salmon. But the trees of the Great Bear Rainforest are a different story. This is an example of what can happen when people like you speak out. It *can* make a difference.

"Today I have grown taller from walking with the trees."
—Karle Wilson Baker, American poet (1878–1960)

Using Wood

Think about all the different ways that you use wood in your own life. Can you name five or even ten off the top of your head? Even if we have never started up a chainsaw or cut down a tree, we all use wood products on a daily basis. We read books and magazines, use toilet paper, live in houses made of wood and sit on chairs made of wood. We write with pencils made of wood on paper that is made from wood, and store our books on wooden bookshelves. We stir our soup with wooden spoons, eat with wooden

OPPOSITE: In and among the salmon rivers and snow-covered mountains live the people, bears and trees of the Great Bear Rainforest. ANDREW S. WRIGHT

TAKE ACTION

Talk to people you disagree with

One of the most important things you can do is talk to the people who are doing something you don't agree with. Often this can seem like the hardest thing in the world. When our families or our friends are making choices that hurt other people, or hurt the Earth, it can be hard to talk to them about it. But if you try, they might learn something from you, and as a result they may make different choices.

One key to talking to people with different opinions is to try and understand things from their perspective. They have reasons for making certain choices in their lives, and nobody likes being told what to do. If you find out more about them and tell them more about yourself, you might discover that even though you have differences, you also share many of the same interests. For example, maybe you think it is wrong that they drive everywhere and never bike or take the bus, but you also know that you both love playing soccer, or you like the same movies. Knowing the things you share can make it easier to talk about difficult topics with somebody and help you stay open to the possibility that they may change your mind also.

"Be passionately aware that you could be completely wrong."
—dian marino, Canadian artist and educator (1941–1993)

chopsticks and dry our hands on paper towels. All of these things are made from trees.

What do you think about trees being cut down so that you can use a paper napkin or paper cup only once before you throw it away? Is it worth cutting down a tree just so that you don't have to do laundry or wash dishes? Is it worth the loss of habitat for birds and wildlife, and for salmon?

Sometimes, it is easy to use less wood. You can use cloth napkins, for example, or reusable mugs. You can reuse your chopsticks and use recycled paper. There are many ways to reduce the number of trees that are cut down.

Using less wood means that more trees can remain standing and more forests can provide habitat for wildlife and places for us to explore. But even if we try hard to use less paper and less wood, we will still need some. In some places, because of the environmental impact of logging, we should stop logging altogether. But this is not the answer everywhere. We have ongoing needs for some wood products, and there are sustainable ways of managing forests that have less of an impact on soil, wildlife and fish.

Walking into a Second-Growth Forest

Remember the old-growth forest you imagined walking into in Chapter 4? Now let's imagine that it was logged and turned into a big clear-cut, and you have come back forty years later to see how the forest has grown back. What grows back after old-growth trees have been logged is called a second-growth forest. Walking into a second-growth forest looks and feels very different from walking into an old-growth forest.

Managed forests are second-growth forests that are planted and thinned and fertilized and sprayed with pesticides, just like a farmer's field. One of the first things you notice when you walk in a managed forest is that the trees are smaller than in an old-growth forest. And the forest looks mostly brown, instead of green. This is because the trees are all the same age, the same size and the same height. The trees grow close together, and very little light gets through their branches. This means that there aren't any berry bushes or other plants on the forest floor because they can't get enough light to grow. Because the trees are so young, they don't have any mosses or lichens or ferns growing on them. Without the nurse logs and **snags** and diversity of plants, there is less habitat available for wildlife. We can still hear kinglets and other birds chirping high up in the canopy, but overall there is much less biodiversity in a planted second-growth forest.

If the forest was left unplanted and allowed to grow back on its own, it would be a very different kind of

Inside a second-growth forest.
MIKE AMBACH

ECO-STORY

Girl in a tree

When I was a young girl, there was a big old cedar tree behind our house. My dad left a ladder leaning up against it so that he and I could reach the lower branches. Climbing up into the tree, sap stuck to my hands and I breathed in the dusty smell of cedar bark. I liked to sit on a branch up near the top and look around, one arm wrapped around the tree so I didn't fall off as it swayed in the wind. From where I was perched, I could see over the tops of the surrounding trees and look out all the way to the ocean.

I find that whenever I feel sad, being outside helps put things into perspective. And what better place than in a tree?

second-growth forest to walk through. At first it would mostly be made up of leafy trees like alders that help bring nutrients into the soil. Many years later you would see small firs and spruce trees growing up under the shade of the alders. If we don't plant trees, it takes longer for the forest to grow big cedar and spruce trees. But if you visited many years later, you would find a healthier forest, with richer soil and a greater diversity of plants and animals.

Logging Moves North

As new technology for logging made it possible to cut trees down faster, the forests along the southern coast of BC were almost all logged. Logging companies began looking toward the central and north coast, where they saw big trees and the potential to make more money. Environmentalists looking at the same area saw intact ecosystems, biodiversity, wildlife and valleys that had never been clear-cut. And the First Nations people who lived in the region saw a place they called home, with valleys they had been living in and harvesting from for thousands of years. They saw people who didn't live in their communities making plans for their land, and they decided that it was high time they had a say in what happened next.

The Environmental Campaign

A map of BC from the 1990s clearly shows two things: most of the coast of BC had already been logged; and there was still one large patch of old-growth forest remaining. Environmentalists named this patch of green the Great Bear Rainforest and

DID YOU KNOW ?

How does a tree grow?

Not only does a tree grow taller each year, it also grows wider. Each year another **growth ring** is added. After a tree has been cut down, you can count the growth rings to find out how old it was.

In years with lots of sun and rain, and in places with rich soil, a tree will grow fast and the growth rings will be widely spaced apart. But if the conditions are poor and the tree is struggling, the growth rings will be very close together. Sometimes they are so small you need a magnifying glass to be able to count them properly. In those years, the tree barely grew any wider.

became determined to prevent clear-cutting from spreading any farther up the coast. They realized that forest companies only make money if people buy their wood products. So environmental groups worked together to launch an international campaign to educate the corporate buyers of wood products about the environmental problems associated with logging in the Great Bear Rainforest. The idea was to convince people to stop buying BC wood until the logging was done more sustainably.

A markets campaign is what it is called when you try to make change by influencing whether certain items are bought or sold. To save the Great Bear Rainforest, environmentalists held rallies and wrote letters and talked to the

TAKE ACTION

Use less paper
Trees that are cut down to make paper once provided homes to birds and wildlife. They held water in the soil and put oxygen into the air. All this was lost so that paper could be made. Do we really need to use so much paper? No doubt we will continue to need some paper, but we could learn to make do with less so that more trees can be left standing. Think about all the paper you use. Are there simple ways to use less? For the paper you absolutely need, could you use recycled paper? Could you organize your school to print less often? Could you wrap gifts in colorful pieces of newspaper, magazines or recycled fabric instead of buying gift wrap?

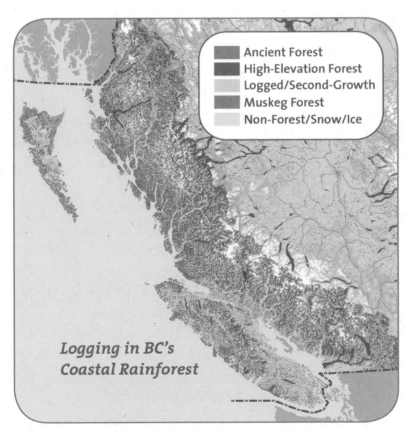

Logging in BC's Coastal Rainforest

Ancient Forest
High-Elevation Forest
Logged/Second-Growth
Muskeg Forest
Non-Forest/Snow/Ice

OPPOSITE (TOP): Greenpeace activists hang from a cargo ship in France to prevent it from unloading timber from Canada's rainforests, 2001. GREENPEACE / PIERRE GLEIZES

OPPOSITE (BOTTOM): Banner on logging machines, Roderick Island, 1997. GREENPEACE / MARK WARFORD

MAP: Much of BC's coast has already been logged, but there are still old-growth forests in the Great Bear Rainforest. SIERRA CLUB BC

companies that were buying wood from BC. They brought these companies on tours to show them clear-cuts of old-growth forests and asked them to consider the environment when deciding what wood products to buy. Around the world, activists dressed up as bears and waved signs,

VOICES FROM THE COAST

Honoring the land

Jess Housty, Heiltsuk First Nation

Jess has been involved in developing management plans for the new protected areas near her home in Bella Bella.

"The new protected areas in the Great Bear Rainforest, called **conservancies**, are special places that we know are safe from logging and other kinds of development. When I walk through a conservancy, I can imagine that, generations from now, my children and grandchildren will also be able to harvest traditional food and medicine plants like I do—like my grandparents taught me to do. If we take care of the land the way our ancestors did, we can honor the land that has sustained us since time before memory, and ensure that these areas are protected into the future.

"Conservancies are different from parks because First Nations have a strong voice in deciding what will happen or not happen in these areas. Also, they are different because the vision for protection includes people. Nature is preserved for its own sake, because it's important to have wild places in our world. The animals are protected too, so they can continue to live a natural existence in balance with one another and their environment. But human values are also protected, and people can continue to interact in meaningful and sustainable ways with the wilderness that exists within our protected areas.

"I feel really lucky, as a young Heiltsuk person, to be involved in figuring out how we can manage and protect our conservancies. When I think about all the people in my life—elders, grandparents, mentors—who have taught me about my roots and my links to the land, it makes me feel good to know I'm helping to preserve the places I love for my nieces and nephews and future generations of Heiltsuk kids!"

holding protests in front of stores and company offices to raise awareness of the environmental impact of clear-cutting in BC. They hung banners with messages about saving ancient rainforests, and they created giant puppets to bring attention to the issue.

It was a campaign that got results: over eighty compa-nies, including IKEA, Home Depot, Staples and IBM, committed to stop selling forest products made from BC's threatened ancient rainforests. The forest companies oper-ating in the Great Bear Rainforest could no longer sell their products. Hundreds of millions of dollars of BC wood sales were at stake. Eventually, in the year 2000, a temporary truce was reached. The environmentalists agreed to stop their protests and the companies agreed to stop logging in large intact valleys and key ecological areas. This truce lasted long enough and provided the basis of trust neces-sary for the people involved to negotiate a new plan for how forestry would happen over the entire area.

The First Nations' Campaign

At the same time that environmental groups were campaigning against logging companies, First Nations were asserting their rights to make decisions about what happens in their traditional territories. They were tired of seeing all the trees cut and logs exported without anyone asking them. They were frustrated that others were making money off the trees from their land, while the people whose land it was weren't benefiting. And they didn't want environmentalists telling them what to do either. First Nations pointed out that they had been governing their land successfully and sustainably for thousands of years. As a result of political pressure, blockades and legal

TOP: Drummers wearing button blanket regalia at a Haida feast.
MIKE AMBACH

BOTTOM: Maps played a key role in the negotiations to protect the Great Bear Rainforest.
SCOTT REHMUS

DID YOU KNOW ?

Wild products from the forest

Apart from wood, there are many other things we make, use or buy that also come from forests. These are called non-timber forest products. Some people find work picking edible mushrooms that grow on the forest floor. These mushrooms are a sought-after delicacy for chefs nearby and far away. Other people harvest ferns and salal branches and sell these as "floral greens" to the flower industry. When you buy flowers, they often come with some ferns or green leaves. Many of these came from the rainforest. Essential oils can be made from conifer tree needles and used in cleaning products or body products like creams and shampoos. Other plants are used for cosmetics, for medicine, or to make teas or jams. When a forest is clear-cut, we get the timber but we lose the possibility of harvesting anything else. With **ecosystem-based management**, more of a forest remains standing and we can continue to harvest these wild products.

Collecting chanterelles (edible mushrooms)
KIKU DHANWANT

MAP: One-third of the Great Bear Rainforest is now protected from logging.

challenges from First Nations, the provincial government no longer has the final say. In the Great Bear Rainforest, land use decisions now have to be made jointly with the First Nation governments.

The Negotiations

What followed the campaigns was years of negotiation. Environmentalists, forest companies, forest workers and tourism operators worked together to try to come up with a solution that everyone could agree on. Eventually, recommendations were made, and then in 2006 the BC government and the First Nations governments reached an agreement.

All these people from different walks of life had to learn how to talk to, respect and get to

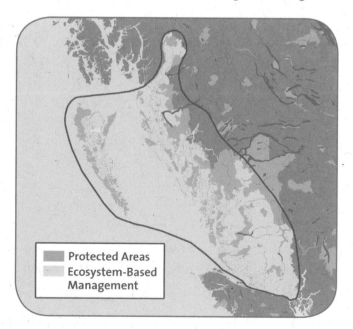

Protected Areas
Ecosystem-Based Management

know each other. If you say to someone, "I'm right and you're wrong," it can be hard to reach agreement. Sometimes this is necessary if somebody is doing something that is entirely unsustainable (like dumping toxic chemicals into the lake your drinking water comes from) and needs to be stopped. But if there is room for compromise, you will only find it if you speak out about what is important to you and why, and then listen to what is important to the people you don't agree with. Then you can figure out a solution together.

The Solution

After the campaigns, the negotiations and the recommendations of scientists, the solution for the Great Bear Rainforest was to set aside one-third of the region in protected areas. This meant that two million hectares (an area three-and-a-half times the size of Prince Edward Island, or slightly larger than the state of New Jersey) was now off-limits to commercial logging. If you dream big, you just may make it happen!

Outside of the protected areas, some logging is allowed but at a reduced rate, and it is to be done in a new way, called ecosystem-based management. This solution shows that it is possible to keep a forest healthy *and* harvest some trees, if it is done carefully.

What is ecosystem-based management?
When settlers first started clearing land in BC, the approach to logging was to take all the trees we wanted. Later, the government regulated how much wood could be harvested. But decisions were primarily based on economics, and environmental values were not taken into consideration. Ecosystem-based management is a new approach that uses science to determine what the ecosystem needs in order to stay healthy. First we ask, "How much do we need to leave behind so that the trees and the wildlife and the birds will survive?" Then we take only whatever amount is available beyond this.

Scientists said that in an intact coastal temperate rainforest, 70 percent of the old-growth trees need to stay standing (along with protection of salmon and wildlife habitat) in order for the rainforest to remain healthy. This means that up to 30 percent of the trees can be harvested, if we make careful decisions about where and how the logging happens. So there are some trees available to get the wood we need, without destroying the forest ecosystem. It is a model that could be applied to salmon harvesting, or to forestry elsewhere in the world, although the science will be different for each situation.

"If we take care of the land, the land will take care of us."
—**April Churchill-Davis,**
Haida Nation, (1951–)

CHAPTER NINE

Driving a Car Through the Rainforest

Okay, so it isn't really possible to drive a car through the rainforest. The forest is so thick that you could never get a car through the three-meter-high (ten-foot) salal bushes and over logs that are a meter or more in diameter! Without a road, driving is clearly impossible. And in most of the Great Bear Rainforest, there are no roads. But driving a car, wherever you live, has an impact on the rainforest. This is because the exhaust from cars is part of what causes climate change.

What Is Climate Change?

Our Earth is surrounded by a thin layer of gases called the **atmosphere**, which is made up of nitrogen, oxygen, argon and the **greenhouse gases** (carbon dioxide, methane and nitrous oxide). The atmosphere is also around each of us— it is the air we breathe. We breathe in oxygen and breathe

"Anything else you're interested in is not going to happen if you can't breathe the air and drink the water. Don't sit this one out. Do something. You are by accident of fate alive at an absolutely critical moment in the history of our planet."
—**Carl Sagan**, American astronomer (1934–1996)

OPPOSITE: Ancient trees are the lungs of the Earth, storing carbon and helping to slow climate change.
ANDREW S. WRIGHT

ABOVE: Plants use the energy from sunlight to make sugars from carbon dioxide, and in the process take carbon out of the atmosphere and store it.
JENS WIETING

OPPOSITE: Scientists predict that climate change will cause a rise in sea level.
CRISTINA MITTERMEIER / iLCP

out carbon dioxide. Plants do the opposite: they take in carbon dioxide and give off oxygen. Carbon dioxide moves through soil, plants, oceans, animals and the atmosphere in a natural cycle that has evolved over millions of years.

When sunlight hits the Earth, some of the heat from the sun gets trapped by the atmosphere and warms our planet. This is called the **greenhouse effect** and it is what makes it possible for us to live on this planet. For the last few thousand years, the amount of carbon dioxide and other greenhouse gases in the atmosphere has stayed relatively stable, keeping the Earth at a mostly constant temperature and allowing life as we know it (plants, animals and human cultures) to flourish.

During the **Industrial Revolution** in the late eighteenth and early nineteenth centuries, we discovered sources of energy that had been buried underground since the time of the dinosaurs. These are called **fossil fuels** and include coal, oil and natural gas. When we burn fossil fuels to heat our homes, power our factories or drive our cars, the burning releases carbon dioxide and other greenhouse gases into the atmosphere.

VOICES FROM THE COAST

Cockles and clams
Linden Fisher (16), Gitga'at First Nation

Linden lives in Hartley Bay, near where a BC ferry sank. *See page 107 for more on this story.*
"The *Queen of the North* is still leaking gas, and it will get in our cockles and clams. That's like poison, and we can die from it. I love cockles—they are yummy fried, steamed and boiled. So are sea cucumbers. Crabs are good with white sauce, and they make good sandwiches."

Trees and oceans can only absorb a certain amount of carbon as part of the natural cycle. This means that when we burn fossil fuels and release additional carbon into the atmosphere, the trees and oceans aren't able to absorb this extra amount of carbon. The more fossil fuels we burn, the more we shift the carbon cycle out of the balance that plants, animals and human cultures have adapted to, and the more carbon accumulates in our atmosphere. This causes extra energy from the sun to get trapped, which makes the Earth heat up. This is called global warming, or climate change.

What Can Be Done About Climate Change?

Our climate is changing. But there is still much that we, as a global society, can do to respond to climate change. If you take action now, you can help ensure that when you grow up you will still be able to enjoy the world more or less as you know it. The two main responses to climate change are **mitigation** and **adaptation**, big words that mean a lot to the world we live in.

Mitigation refers to actions we take in order to stop causing climate change. Climate change has already begun, but we can still slow it down so the impact isn't as severe. To do this, we need to reduce the amount of greenhouse gases being released into our atmosphere. For example, we can reduce fossil fuel emissions by driving less and taking the train instead of flying, where possible.

DID YOU KNOW

What does climate change mean to you?

As a result of increasing amounts of carbon dioxide in the atmosphere, the Earth is warming up. But this doesn't necessarily mean that the Earth will suddenly be a tropical paradise. In some places it might be uncomfortably hot. And in some places it might actually be colder than it is now.

With warmer temperatures, the polar ice caps are melting. This will raise sea levels worldwide. Climate change will also cause more extreme weather patterns, such as floods, droughts, hurricanes, heat waves and blizzards. And animals are showing up in unexpected places. For example, Humboldt squid, fierce predators that can grow up to 2 meters (6.5 feet) in length, are usually found in warmer waters, but they have been seen in the ocean off the Great Bear Rainforest and are washing up on beaches in the hundreds. What are scientists predicting will happen as a result of climate change where you live?

TAKE ACTION

Making a difference for our climate

Fifteen-year-old Vamsi Chatapuram of Vancouver, BC, sees the connections between his actions and climate change. He rides his bike everywhere and often debates and challenges his classmates on environmental issues. Because of his concern for the environment, Vamsi plays a key role in composting and gardening projects at his school. He is a member of the Eco Power Green Team, a group of students who are growing food plants in the empty areas around the school. "I am involved in the project because I think it would be awesome if we grow our own food and don't ship in much food from elsewhere." He says that these changes to his school are important because "they are the first step to getting people to start being eco-friendly. They are also the first steps for the school to be less wasteful and less dependent on getting food from other sources." At his previous school in India, Vamsi planted a tamarind tree because he likes eating tamarinds and because the tree has edible leaves. Here in Canada, he keeps asking his teachers why they don't plant part of the school field with trees for carbon storage and wildlife habitat.

Vamsi Chatapuram. KARTHIK CHATAPURAM

Adaptation refers to actions we take to make the changing climate easier to live with. Every plant and animal is dependent on particular conditions of light, temperature, food sources and water availability. If the changing climate affects any of these conditions, the plant or animal may need to migrate in order to survive. For example, if their habitat becomes too warm or too cold, they will try to move to another place where the temperature is just right. To make this possible, we need to protect enough wild spaces so that species have room to move.

The Great Bear Rainforest Can Help!

Protecting old-growth forests in the Great Bear Rainforest will help to ensure that the salmon, the bears and other creatures will have somewhere to go if the changing climate makes it intolerable to live in other parts of the coast.

But the rainforest also helps prevent climate change. How does this work? As a tree grows, it takes carbon out of the atmosphere and turns it into wood. The older a forest is, the more carbon is stored in the trunks and branches of the big trees. When trees die and fall over, the carbon is stored in the soil. Old-growth forests contain huge amounts of carbon.

If a forest is logged, a small amount of carbon is stored in the wood products, but most of the carbon that was stored in trees and in the soil is released into the atmosphere. This means that choosing *not* to log is an important way to prevent the release of greenhouse gases.

In this way, climate change connects all of us to the Great Bear Rainforest. All of us live under the same sky, breathe the same air and share the same atmosphere. The old-growth trees in the Great Bear Rainforest benefit everyone on Earth by playing a role in storing carbon and helping to slow climate change. The same is true of the boreal forest and the Amazon rainforest and other large intact forests around the world.

> *"When we plant trees, we plant the seeds of peace and seeds of hope."*
> —Wangari Maathai, Nobel Peace Prize winner (1940–)

ECO-STORY

Pulling my head out of the sand

For years I have volunteered and worked as an environmental activist. But when it comes to climate change, I am the first to admit I have been in denial. I knew climate change was a problem, but it seemed too big and too scary. I was busy with other projects, and I didn't know what I could do.

Globally, climate change is predicted to cause massive droughts, sea-level rise and extinction of between 15 and 37 percent of all land-based animals and plants. The oceans are acidifying: shellfish will no longer be able to properly form their shells. Crop yields will decrease, there will be food shortages, people will die and millions of people will be displaced from their homes. It's overwhelming. What is a person supposed to *do* with all this information?

It's a lot to try and hold in my mind, in my heart. It's hard to stay present, to not push it away and go back to pretending everything is fine. Everything *isn't* fine, and I think deep down we all know that. So then the question for me is, what do I do? I decided to get involved. I participated in a **flash mob** dance that was performed on an international day of action on climate change. It was fun, and I felt part of something bigger, but I wanted to do more. So I helped organize a **sit-in**. We occupied the office of an elected government representative for a day to ask the Canadian government to do more to stop climate change. We organized a rally and marched through the streets with banners, chants and songs. I found my voice, speaking into a megaphone. We didn't change government policy that day, but it felt incredibly important to speak out and to build up a movement of people willing to take action on climate change.

TAKE ACTION

A high school goes solar!

A group of students at a high school in Victoria, BC, raised the money needed to install solar panels on their school roof. The project emerged out of a brainstorming session during a grade-nine science class, when each student was asked to design a "green" high school. Their teacher noticed that many of the students wanted solar panels for the school to provide a portion of the school's electrical needs. He encouraged them to pursue this dream, and the Oak Bay Solar Panel Project was born.

At first it was hard to believe that they could possibly be successful. The system they wanted to install cost more than thirty-thousand dollars, and they only had seven students in the group, most without any fundraising experience.

The group started by making a video about their project and presenting it to the school at an assembly. Then they set up displays and collected hundreds of dollars at local community events, and distributed hundreds more student-designed stickers and business cards promoting their cause. Still, thirty-thousand dollars was a lot of money to raise! They started applying for grants from the government and approaching local businesses for their support. Over the course of the project, the group was featured on almost every local radio station and many television stations, as well as in articles published in both local and national papers. Finally, after a year ▶▶

Continued on page 107

The Great Bear Rainforest: At risk

Some of the activities that are causing climate change pose a threat to the Great Bear Rainforest. The coastline of BC is laced with long narrow fjords. Being in a boat in these fjords can be treacherous in stormy weather. And yet, some governments and businesses would like to see oil tankers as long as three football fields traveling up and down these narrow channels. The chances of an oil spill would be high, and many of the First Nations and other people who live on the coast don't think it is worth the risk.

An Oil Spill to Remember

One night in March 1989, the *Exxon Valdez* oil tanker ran aground on a rocky reef in Alaska. It was carrying oil from Alaska to feed the cars and industries of the United States. Sharp rocks ripped the side of the tanker open; the oil that spilled out would have filled 125 Olympic-size swimming pools!

It was an environmental disaster. Birds coated in oil were no longer able to keep themselves warm, and they couldn't fly. Sea otters depend on their fur to stay warm, so when they were covered in oil, they literally froze to death. The otters and birds also swallowed the oil when trying to clean themselves, and they died when the oil poisoned them from the inside. The oil affected the plankton, which are food for the salmon and the herring. The whales and animals and birds that eat herring and salmon also became contaminated with oil, and many died.

The oil spill was also a disaster for the people who made their living from the sea. There were fewer fish to catch, and no one wanted to buy or eat seafood contaminated with oil. The processing plants and canneries closed, and many people lost their jobs. The First Nations were no longer able to eat the fish, shellfish, waterfowl and wild animals they depended on for food.

Even after a massive clean-up effort, oil from the spill that happened over twenty years ago still washes up on shores 700 kilometers (435 miles) away and could take centuries to disappear. The communities and coastal ecosystems have not recovered.

The *Exxon Valdez* disaster taught us that an oil spill can cause severe and lasting damage to the rainforest and coastal ecosystems. In 2010, the blowout of the BP Deepwater Horizon oil well in the Gulf of Mexico was a reminder that accidents are bound to happen (even with the best modern technology) and that cleanup is next to impossible, and coastal communities suffer as jobs in fishing and tourism are lost.

Why would anyone contemplate sending oil tankers through the world's largest remaining intact coastal temperate rainforest? The reason: we live in a society that is addicted to oil. We use oil to drive our cars, grow our food, make our clothes, make plastic and heat our homes. Many household items are made using oil, including toothbrushes, plastic milk jugs, toys, running shoes, garden hoses and telephones. Canada's **tar sands** are a source of oil, and tankers moving through the rainforest would bring oil from the tar sands to the United States and Asia, where it could be used to drive cars, heat homes and make more household products for us to buy.

Gitga'at People to the Rescue

The Gitga'at people of Hartley Bay sleep with their marine radios on. And it's a good thing they do. In the middle

TAKE ACTION

▶▶ *Continued from page 106*
of hard work, they had raised enough money. In 2009 the ten solar panels arrived at the school and were lifted by crane onto the roof. A media event was organized to celebrate the success of the first entirely student-run solar project in BC. The panels were dedicated to the power of student initiative.

Student activists who brought solar panels to their school.

Dead loon found in Kenai Fjords, Alaska, after the *Exxon Valdez* oil spill disaster, 1989. GREENPEACE/KEN GRAHAM

TAKE ACTION

Reduce your dependence on oil

One simple way to reduce your dependence on oil is to use less plastic. Take a cloth bag to the store instead of asking for a plastic bag. Fill up a reusable water bottle with tap water instead of buying water in plastic bottles. Consuming less stuff overall reduces not only your **carbon footprint** but also your ecological footprint. Instead of birthday gifts, some kids ask that donations be given to a cause. Other families exchange homemade presents for Christmas, Hanukkah or other holidays. What can you do to reduce the amount of plastic stuff you or your family buys?

ABOVE: Boats from this dock in Hartley Bay rescued passengers from the *Queen of the North*.
CAITLYN VERNON

RIGHT: Alberta's tar sands used to be boreal forest.
GREENPEACE / COLIN O'CONNER

of a March night in 2006, the village was woken up by a desperate call for help on the radio. The *Queen of the North*, a BC ferry carrying 101 passengers and their cars from Prince Rupert to Vancouver Island, had struck an island not far away and was sinking. Everyone with a boat rushed off in the rain and darkness to rescue the survivors, who were bobbing around in lifeboats in the choppy waves. Back in town, the entire village pitched in to do what they could to look after the crew and passengers when they were brought to shore. Children gathered blankets, clothes and shoes and even did media interviews in the middle of the night. Two people were never found, but thanks to the quick response from the people of Hartley Bay, everyone else survived.

The heroes of the rescue now live with the legacy of that sunken ferry. The diesel and oil that was on board coated approximately 89 kilometers (55 miles) of coastline, killed hundreds of birds, and contaminated shellfish in the area. The Gitga'at people now have to travel

farther to gather clams, mussels, sea cucumbers, sea urchins and prawns. They also worry about the contamination of crabs and seaweed and the effects of the ongoing seepage of fuel on herring, salmon, seals, sea lions and whales.

The Gitga'at know what an oil spill looks like and how it smells. While the spill from the *Queen of the North* has had a major impact, the amount of diesel leaking from the ferry is small compared to the two million barrels of oil that a super-tanker can carry. From where it lies at the bottom of the ocean, the *Queen of the North* is a constant reminder that accidents do happen to big ships on the coast.

Tar Sands and Tankers

Alberta's tar sands are Canada's biggest source of greenhouse gas emissions: they generate more emissions than all the cars in Canada combined. What are these tar sands, and what do they have to do with the Great Bear Rainforest?

Buried under the boreal forests and wetlands of northern Alberta is a type of fossil fuel called bitumen. Once extracted from the ground, this tar-like substance needs to undergo energy-intensive processing and refining to turn it into oil and make it thin enough to flow through pipes. As of 2010, refining the tar sands uses more water every day than a city of two million people and consumes enough natural gas to heat six million Canadian homes. The process creates enormous lakes full of toxic chemicals, contaminates rivers

DID YOU KNOW

How does turning off the lights make a difference?
Turning out the lights when you leave a room can help mitigate climate change. To understand how this works, you have to follow the electricity back to where it is produced. In many parts of North America, electricity is generated by burning fossil fuels. Oil, coal and natural gas are burned in power plants to generate the electricity that turns your lights on. So saving electricity by turning out the lights helps keep fossil fuels in the ground and reduces the amount of greenhouse gases released into the atmosphere.

If your electricity comes from hydro power, saving energy is still a good thing, because it means that fewer rivers need to be dammed and fewer valleys flooded. Even if you use solar or wind power, saving energy means that fewer resources need to go into building solar panels and windmills.

Some people say that new technology is the answer to climate change. It is convenient to think that new technologies will provide all the energy we need so that we don't have to make any changes in our own lives. And it's true that some technologies, like wind and solar, are an important part of a more sustainable future. But when we remember that the Earth is a finite ecosystem in which there is limited availability of the resources and energy required to build technologies like windmills and solar panels, it becomes clear that conservation is the most important action we can take. Assessing how much energy and resources we *really* need, and learning to live with less, will show the leadership required to respond to climate change. So even with the promise of new technologies, turning off the lights (and encouraging friends, family and political leaders to conserve energy also) is important.

TAKE ACTION

No tankers

When grandmother Helen Clifton from the Gitga'at First Nation thinks about the tankers that might travel right in front of the village of Hartley Bay, she says she feels a sense of impending doom. "You've got to struggle to rise above it," she says, "and fight with all you've got."

Many people, up and down the coast of BC, are speaking up to keep tankers out of the Great Bear Rainforest. People are making their voices heard in creative ways: signing petitions, joining rallies, making videos, writing letters to the editors of newspapers, taking photographs of the region to show the world all that would be lost with an oil spill, even putting stickers onto the Canadian one-dollar coin that show the loon covered in oil. One man traveled by stand-up paddleboard along the proposed tanker route (in up to 7-meter or 22-foot waves!) to raise awareness and get more people involved.

And the coastal First Nations have issued a strong declaration, banning tankers from traveling through their traditional territories. First Nations and others on the coast are speaking from the heart when they say *no* to tankers and *yes* to healthy ecosystems and healthy coastal communities.

IAN MCALLISTER

and groundwater, destroys boreal forests and releases air pollution. Downstream from the tar sands, wildlife has disappeared, fish are strangely mutated and people are experiencing high rates of rare cancers.

If this is such a dirty process, why bother? The thing is, other sources of oil around the world are being used up to fuel our cars and airplanes and factories. In order to keep everything running smoothly, oil companies are always searching for new sources of oil. And even though extracting oil from the tar sands is not easy and leaves an environmental mess behind, it is possible and there is money to be made. The tar sands pump out over one million barrels of oil every single day. Pipelines from Alberta to the rest of North America bring oil to your doorstep (and sometimes spill oil along the way, contaminating rivers and wildlife habitat). To get more oil to more doorsteps, proposed new pipelines would bring oil to the coast, where it would be shipped in tankers through the narrow fjords of the Great Bear Rainforest.

We are all a part of this. The more time we spend driving in cars, and the more plastic stuff we buy, the more pressure there is on the Alberta tar sands to produce oil, and the more likely it is that we will see oil tankers and oil spills in the rainforest. That means that we all have a chance to make a difference. If we take action at home or at school to reduce our use of fossil fuels, we are doing two things. First, we are helping to prevent climate change by lowering our greenhouse gas emissions. And second, we are reducing our dependence on oil. In a future where we use less oil, we don't need the tar sands and we don't have to ship oil tankers through the rainforest. Once again, we can choose what future we want to live in.

Picturing the future

When I try to picture what sort of future I want for myself, and for any children and grandchildren I might have one day, I don't see tar sands or tankers. I see a future where we have made a choice to stop burning so much oil. Our climate will be different than it is today; there will be impacts of climate change that we need to adjust to and live with. But there will be big trees in the rainforest, salmon in the ocean, marmots in high alpine meadows, and most of the wildlife species I have come to love will still exist. We will have made a choice—before it was too late, before the increasing temperatures led to catastrophic changes in our world—to stop releasing the greenhouse gases that are heating up our atmosphere.

And what does this future actually look like on a regular day? Will there be cars or just horses and buggies? That depends on choices we make today. The amount of available fossil fuel is finite. In other words, there is only a limited amount in the earth, and once we use it up, it is gone for good. If we continue on as we are and use up all the remaining oil in the ground, not only will our climate change significantly, but we will also be forced to live without any of the conveniences that oil provides. Because it will all be gone. I call this the "all we want now, but nothing later" scenario.

Or we can choose to reduce our dependence on fossil fuels immediately. That will help prevent the worst of the climate change and has the added bonus of allowing us the use of some oil to transition to a new way of life. We can use the remaining fossil fuels carefully over time, and build, for example, solar panels and windmills so we still have sources of energy. This is the "less now, some later" scenario.

Either way, we are facing a future without oil. And you know what? If we make the transition now, that future looks pretty good! People will live in small communities where they can walk or bike to school and to visit their friends. Everyone eats **organic food** grown locally, and more people are farmers. We dry our clothes on clotheslines with the heat of the sun and the power of the wind. Decisions are made that put people and the health of the environment first, before profit. There are electric cars, and if you want to travel, you take the train or a bus. Forestry is done sustainably, providing wood and paper for our use but leaving large areas of forest undisturbed. Fish are caught using techniques that ensure the health and survival of the fisheries. Our "stuff" is made with care and is built to last. We live in a way that respects the ecological limits of what the Earth can provide and what amount of waste it can deal with. We care for each other, and we care for the Earth.

CAITLYN VERNON

CHAPTER TEN

A Time for Action

Many species and ecosystems are in bad shape, but their story isn't over yet. There is still hope. Bringing them back to good health is a real possibility. It has happened before and it can happen again. Dirty rivers become clean, species like the sea otters return to the ocean, tanker traffic is stopped. And that's because people have chosen to take action on environmental issues. You too can become part of the solution! Through your actions, you can inspire others around you to follow your lead.

How to begin? Get informed, make careful choices, get inspired and get involved.

"Now I know that if you believe in something strongly enough, you can make things change. No matter what your age."
—**Robyn Eliason** (12), Environmental activist (from *It's Our World, Too!* by Phillip Hoose)

OPPOSITE: Ravens make a wide range of noises, from knocking sounds and gurgling croaks to rasping alarm calls. They will sometimes imitate the sounds of people and other birds.
DOUGLAS NEASLOSS

Get Informed

Each place is different. Each place will have a different definition of sustainability that works for the ecosystems

TAKE ACTION

The woman who lived in a tree

Have you ever slept in a tree? A woman named Julia Butterfly Hill has. She actually *lived* in a tree for two years. She was trying to prevent ancient redwood trees in California from being logged. As long as she was in the tree, no one would cut it down or log nearby. Julia was determined to stay in the tree until it was protected from logging. It took a long time, but with the help of many people on the ground, eventually the tree was saved. You can read her amazing story in the book called *The Legacy of Luna.*

ABOVE: Giant salmon puppet on wheels. JENS WIETING

RIGHT: A young mother grizzly guards her two cubs. ANDREW S. WRIGHT

and the people who live in them. Find out what is being proposed for where you live. What kinds of forestry, fishery and renewable energy are possible where you live? What food is grown locally? Are there people working to protect endangered wildlife, or to establish new protected areas on land or in the ocean? Are the First Nations and other people who live in the area involved in determining what the environmental solutions should be?

Are there youth in your community who are taking action on environmental issues? Does your school have an environment committee? Are there any environmental organizations in your town or city that are run by youth?

Make Careful Choices

Our actions have consequences. If we understand the impacts of our actions, we can make wise choices for the future of our planet. The choices we make—what food

Finding hope

On the days when I struggle to find hope, it gives me some comfort to know that even if we make really bad decisions, the natural world is incredibly resilient and some form of life will continue. Humans are just a small blip in the big picture of life on Earth, and even though we have a huge impact, there is no question in my mind that life will go on. Watching spirit bears fish for salmon in the Great Bear Rainforest gives me hope that the magical cycle of salmon will continue long into the future.

I feel more hopeful when I look to the courage and creativity of people all around the world who are standing up to demand—and create—a more sustainable future. I am inspired by everyone who is making change happen in their own life: organic farmers, committed cyclists, people who power their homes with renewable energy, groups who daylight a salmon stream in their urban backyard, neighbors who come together to grow food on their urban boulevards, people who fight to save the last of the ancient rainforest trees. And I am inspired and motivated by those individuals who risk arrest to raise awareness about the environmental issues we are facing. They remind us, with banner drops, sit-ins, blockades and other forms of direct action, to think about what is really at stake.

The days when I feel the most hopeful are the days when I am surrounded by hundreds (sometimes even thousands!) of people who see the environmental challenges we are facing and are willing to do something about them. There are small-scale local changes that we can all make, but there also need to be bigger political and economic changes to how we make decisions as a society. It is among massive mobilizations of people that I feel most hopeful that these broader changes will happen. When I look to the past, I find inspiration from historical struggles and the successes that were won. It certainly wasn't easy gaining the rights that we now take for granted—votes for women, racial equality—and many people sacrificed a lot in the process. But addressing the climate change challenge today is going to require that same degree of motivation and mobilization. Looking to history gives me hope that we can do this!

Rally at the BC legislature.
JENS WIETING

TAKE ACTION

Carbon footprints

The idea of a carbon footprint arose from the concept of calculating your ecological footprint. Your ecological footprint is the amount of land and sea that is required to generate all the resources you consume and absorb all of the waste that you produce. Your carbon footprint is the amount of greenhouse gas emissions generated by your household. In a climate-changing world, if we understand which aspects of our lifestyle produce the most greenhouse gases, then we can take action to reduce our emissions.

There are greenhouse gas emissions related to how you get around, what you eat, what you buy, how you heat your home, how much garbage you produce, how much hot water you use and how many electronic gadgets you own. Reducing your emissions can come from making changes to your lifestyle and adjusting the purchasing choices of your family. Many small actions can help, such as turning off your computer (and monitor) when you're not using it, and riding your bike or taking the bus instead of asking to be driven somewhere. There are lots of calculators online to help you calculate your carbon footprint and find ways to reduce it.

As individuals and with our families, our actions and choices can and do make a difference. But climate change is a big global problem that requires a big global response. As we make changes in our own lives, we also need to encourage our ▸▸

Continued on page 117

we eat, how we get around, how much stuff we buy—have an impact on the Great Bear Rainforest and other ecosystems. There are simple things we can do, like finding ways to use less paper, that make a big difference.

Once you know where stuff comes from, you can decide if you really need it. Maybe you don't...or maybe there is a more sustainable alternative.

Get Inspired

Learning about all the problems in the world can feel overwhelming. It can help to hear about all the people who are working to make a difference, and to know there are other people out there who share your concerns. It can be inspiring to learn about the creative actions they

Take time to enjoy this amazing world we live in. MIKE AMBACH

are taking to make this world a better place for all of us to live in.

What gives you hope? What inspires you? When days are hard and you feel frustrated and alone, search for those people and ideas and places that inspire you. Find the good news stories. Hold on to them in your mind. Keep dreaming of the future you want to see. Remember that there are many fabulous people out there who care, who are working hard and who have made a difference.

Get Involved

Are you concerned about something that is happening in the world or in your community? You've learned more about it, and now you want to do something. But what? There are many different ways to get involved. One way isn't better than another way; they are all valuable. You can decide what feels best for you.

Find an issue that you are passionate about so that you bring energy and commitment to whatever you do. Then decide whether you want to join in an existing campaign or organization, organize a group yourself or take action on your own.

Speak Up, Dance, Organize

Where to begin? Assess the issue you are concerned about and decide if the solution can happen at home or at school, or if it requires a broader community and government response. Then plan your strategies accordingly so your message reaches the people who need to hear it most. Here are some ideas for action to get you started.

TAKE ACTION

▶▶ Continued from page 116

governments to do what is necessary to reduce the carbon footprint of our entire country. We need solutions that match the scale of the problem. Switching to energy-efficient lightbulbs is important, but this action by itself isn't going to stop climate change. There are many things our governments could do to better address the scale of the problem we are facing: for example, regulate industries so they have to reduce their greenhouse gas emissions, end the subsidies that make fossil fuels appear cheaper than they really are, do more to encourage public transportation, and provide incentives for families and businesses to make their homes and offices more energy efficient so that less energy is required.

Responding to the challenges of a changing climate requires leadership and creativity from everyone involved: from our own choices to conserve energy and drive less, to government laws and regulations that require industries to reduce their emissions and make energy conservation more possible, to international treaties in which we commit to working with other countries to take action on climate change. Remember, you can make your voice heard at all of these levels, and there is power in speaking out.

TOP: Who says dinosaurs can't ride bikes? WAYNE WORDEN

BOTTOM: Kids have voices too! MAGGIE ZIEGLER

1. Start a group at your school to learn more about a topic, and brainstorm ways to make a difference
2. Run for student council to advocate for the changes you'd like to see happen in your school
3. Volunteer for an environmental organization
4. Make your voice heard: write letters to your local politicians or go and talk to them in their office; write letters to your local newspapers; post comments online; call in to radio talk shows; set up an information booth on the street and talk to people; sing songs; use Facebook and Twitter
5. Organize an event, invite an inspiring guest speaker and encourage everyone who attends to get involved in some way
6. Organize a letter-writing campaign, or start a petition
7. Raise money to support a campaign; hold a walk-a-thon or bike-a-thon as a fundraiser
8. Create a community mural
9. Organize a Critical Mass bike ride (Critical Mass is a bicycling event typically held on the last Friday of every month in over three hundred cities around the world)
10. Talk to your local supermarkets and restaurants about selling sustainable seafood. If necessary, organize a boycott to encourage a company to stop (or start) selling certain products
11. Be creative. There are many ways of making change: do artwork; write poetry; get your sports team involved
12. Organize a flash mob, start a group of radical cheerleaders, or write new words for old chants and songs
13. Make videos or record songs and post them on YouTube, or make a radio documentary

14. Do a theatre performance in a public space to raise awareness about your issue
15. Lobby your local government to make your town or city more bike-friendly or skateboard-friendly
16. Organize a youth rally so young people can speak out
17. Start a vegetable garden at your school
18. Compost your fruit and vegetable scraps (in a backyard compost bin or a worm bin in your classroom)
19. Become a streamkeeper. Plant trees along salmon streams to restore spawning habitat
20. Hold a film festival on a specific topic that concerns you
21. Hold a competition at your school to see who can go the longest without using a disposable cup or buying bottled water
22. Encourage everyone in your neighborhood to stop receiving junk mail
23. Publish an environmental newsletter or write a blog
24. Organize a field trip to a farm or a local windmill to learn more

Above all, do something you enjoy. The issues are serious, but working to make change doesn't have to be dull or boring. You can make it fun!

Whatever you do, it is important that you don't try to do everything at once. Often, when we are concerned about the world, we take too much on and try to save it all. No one person can do everything. It's important to take care of yourself at the same time, and whatever you choose to do, make sure you have a good time doing it!

TOP: High school students organized a climate-change bike relay, along with an eco-fair, live music and local food, to raise money to install solar panels on their school. BRIAN VAN WYK

BOTTOM: Youth Action Gathering, building leadership and organizing skills for environmental and social justice. SIERRA YOUTH COALITION

"Tell me, what is it you plan to do with your one wild and precious life?"
—Mary Oliver, American poet (1935–)

The raven

One day I was walking along the edge of a cliff above a big river. A raven followed me along the trail, landing on tree branches and calling to me. At a place along the cliff where the air currents formed strong updrafts, the raven started to play. When wind hits a cliff, the air shoots upward so strongly that a bird can get carried up without having to flap its wings. The raven soared upward effortlessly. Then, at the top, it flipped over, tucked its wings in and dived straight down, spiraling as it went. After a few long seconds of spinning free fall, the raven caught the updraft and soared back up to the top. It did this again and again as I stood there laughing, wishing that I too could play in the wind.

Sometimes, if I am quiet and stop to listen, the Earth will remind me of all the beauty and life that is out there. Whenever this happens, I feel inspired to keep doing the work I do, to try and protect this piece of the coast for future generations to enjoy. And I am reminded of how interconnected we all are to this natural world we call home.

These moments happen unexpectedly. The stench of whale breath coming off the ocean through the fog. A glimpse of a spirit bear, its dirty white fur all soggy in the pouring rain that has soaked me also. Watching the magical mystery of salmon returning to the very same stream they were born in. The smell of cedar bark after a rain. Realizing that the Heiltsuk word for eagle sounds a bit like the eagle's call.

These moments happen in the city too. Noticing a tomato plant growing through a crack in a downtown sidewalk. Waking up to the sound of baby birds chirping from nests in my neighbor's walls. Weeds that come back, again and again, persistently bringing green to barren spaces. Watching leaves float down in lazy circles from the branches up above.

There is no getting around it. As much as any other animal, we humans depend on the natural world for our survival. And because we have such a big impact, the health of the natural world depends on us. We have a choice about how we want the story to end. As activist and writer Arundhati Roy once said, "Another world is possible...On a quiet day, I can hear her breathing."

CAITLYN VERNON

OPPOSITE: Breathing it in. TJ WATT

Glossary

adaptation—(a) in the context of climate change, refers to actions we take to make humans and other species less vulnerable to, and more prepared for, the changing climate; (b) in the context of evolution, refers to gradual changes in structure, function or behavior over many generations by which a species improves its chance of survival in a specific environment

amphibian—a type of animal whose young (called tadpoles) are born in water and breathe with gills, then transform into adults that live mostly on land and breathe through lungs and their skin

aquaculture—the cultivation (farming) of fish or shellfish for human consumption or use

assembly line—a line of factory workers and equipment along which a product being assembled passes consecutively from operation to operation until completed

atmosphere—a layer of gases that surrounds the Earth, made up of nitrogen, oxygen, argon and the greenhouses gases (carbon dioxide, methane and nitrous oxide)

backcasting—the process of visualizing the future you want to see and then working backward to figure out what steps are necessary to take today in order to make that future possible

baleen—the comb-like structures that some whales have in their mouths to filter plankton from seawater when feeding. Baleen is made from keratin, the same substance that is in hair, nails and horns

big house—a large wooden building used by First Nations for cultural events and community gatherings, typically with a fireplace in the middle, drummers at one end, a carved pole in each corner and places to sit along the sides

biodiversity—the diversity of plants and animals living within a specific ecosystem. An area with many different kinds of plants and animals has "high biodiversity." Biodiversity is often used as an indicator of a healthy ecosystem

boreal forest—a type of coniferous forest that is found in areas where the winters are long and cold and the trees grow very slowly. Boreal forest covers 35 percent of Canada and is also found in Russia, Sweden, Finland and Norway

carbon footprint—a calculation that assesses how human activities are contributing to climate change by measuring the amount of greenhouse gas emissions generated by our food, energy use, transportation choices and the stuff we buy

carnivores—animals that feed on other animals

celestial navigation—using the position of the stars to find your way

Chinook Jargon—a simplified language created by fur traders and First Nations on the northwest coast of North America so they could talk to each other, made up of words from English, French and First Nation languages. The language is no longer spoken, although some words are still commonly used

clear-cut—a type of logging that removes all the trees from the forest, either in small or large areas

climate—the general or average weather conditions of a certain region, including temperature, rainfall and wind; affected by latitude (how far north or south the region is located), altitude (how high), and proximity (how close) to the ocean

climate change—variations in the climate as the composition of greenhouse gases in the atmosphere changes in response to the effects of volcanic eruptions, ocean temperature and circulation patterns, and human activities that release greenhouse gases. *See also* global warming; greenhouse effect

coastal temperate rainforest—a rare type of forest known for its large ancient trees and high amounts of rainfall, located next to the ocean in temperate (moderate) climates and characterized by complex interactions between land and sea ecosystems

colonization—when one country or group of people move into another territory and take it over, generally without the support or agreement of the people who already live there

conservancies—a type of protected area, different from a park, where land is set aside for the protection of ecosystems, recreational opportunities and culture, while allowing some low-impact uses by First Nations

deciduous forest—a forest composed primarily of deciduous trees, which lose their leaves in the fall and grow new leaves in the spring, compared to evergreen trees, which stay green year-round

decompose—the process by which dead plants or animals are broken down into smaller pieces by millipedes, slugs, insects, bacteria or fungi

echolocation—the sonar-like system used by whales and bats to navigate (find their way) and find food

ecological footprint—a calculation that assesses the impact humans are having on the Earth by measuring the amount of land and ocean that is required to generate all the resources we consume (such as food, energy, minerals, wood, water, etc.) and absorb all of the waste that we produce (garbage, greenhouse gas emissions, etc.)

ecosystem—a community of plants and animals, living together with their physical environment

ecosystem-based management—a way to make decisions about how many trees we can cut down or fish we can harvest, while still maintaining the health of the ecosystem we are harvesting from, by first asking what the ecosystem needs in order to survive and then only taking what is available beyond this

endangered species—a plant or animal species existing in such small numbers that it is in danger of becoming extinct, often as a result of over-harvesting or loss of habitat

estuary—the area where a river meets the sea, characterized by rich soil and a mix of fresh and salt water; important habitat for many species of fish and wildlife

evaporate—to convert a liquid into a gas. For example, when sunlight warms the surface of the ocean, water evaporates and rises into the air as something called water vapor, which is what forms clouds

evolution—the gradual change in the characteristics of a population of animals or plants over successive generations, which can lead to the emergence of new species

extinction—the complete elimination of a species to the point that there are no live examples of the particular plant or animal left anywhere in the world

filter feeders—an aquatic animal, such as a clam or barnacle or baleen whale, that feeds by filtering tiny animals or particles of food out of the water

finite—having limitations. For example, ecosystems are finite, with natural limits that restrict the availability of resources (trees, food, water, etc.) and the ability to absorb waste

First Nations—distinct groups of people who have lived all across North America since before European colonization, each with their own language, culture and government

fjords—long and narrow inlets, formed by glaciers, that stretch far inland, with steep mountains on either side

flash mob—a group of people who meet at a predetermined time in a public place, perform something unexpected like a dance or a song, and then all quickly disperse without talking to each other. Generally done for entertainment, to reclaim public space, and/or to spread a political message

fossil fuels—sources of energy, such as coal, oil and natural gas, formed by plants and animals, that decomposed and were buried underground hundreds of millions of years ago, before the time of the dinosaurs

fungi (*sing.* fungus)—a type of organism, neither plant nor animal, that lives by decomposing and absorbing the organic material on which it grows

global warming—the heating up of our global atmosphere, causing sea-level rise and an increase in extreme weather patterns, as a result of human activities that release greenhouse gases.

An example of extremely rapid climate change. *See also* greenhouse effect

greenhouse effect—the natural process by which heat from the sun gets trapped in our atmosphere and warms the Earth. Also the process that leads to global warming, as more greenhouse gases accumulate in the atmosphere and more heat is trapped

greenhouse gases—the gases in our atmosphere, including carbon dioxide, methane and nitrous oxide, that trap heat from the sun in the greenhouse effect. Human activities, such as the burning of fossil fuels, are increasing the amount of greenhouse gases in our atmosphere

growth ring—an indication of the amount that a tree grows in a given year, formed because a tree grows faster in the spring than at other times of year. Visible in a cross-section of a tree after it has been cut down. The number of rings can be counted to determine the age of the tree

habitat—the place or environment where a plant or animal usually lives, characterized by features such as type of soil, temperature, amount of rainfall, as well as the presence of food, shelter and other plants and animals

hibernation—an inactive state resembling deep sleep in which certain animals, such as bears, pass the winter. In hibernation, the breathing and heart rates slow down and the animals survive on body fat built up during the summer and fall when food was plentiful

hydrophone—a device used to detect or monitor sounds underwater, such as the sounds made by whales

Indian reserves—the small parcels of land that First Nations, who had formerly occupied much larger areas, were restricted to and made to live on so that European settlers could open the rest of the land up for settlement, farming, forestry and mining

Industrial Revolution—a period of rapid industrialization during the late eighteenth and early nineteenth centuries, fueled by the increased burning of fossil fuels to generate energy, during which people shifted from making and doing things by hand to using machines and making things in factories

intertidal zone—the area between the land and sea that is covered by water at high tide and uncovered at low tide

magnetic compass—a device used to determine geographical direction based on the Earth's magnetic field

managed forests—second-growth forests that have been planted with young trees and are sometimes thinned, fertilized and sprayed with pesticides

markets campaign—a type of campaign that tries to encourage political or economic changes by influencing whether certain items are bought or sold; for example, by educating customers to boycott (stop buying from) businesses that are damaging ecosystems or exploiting workers in the process of making their products

mass-produce—to manufacture something in large quantities, often with extensive mechanization and/or assembly-line techniques

mechanization—when machines are introduced into a process that was formerly done with manual labor

microorganism—an organism too small to be viewed with just the human eye, that can only be seen with the help of a microscope

mitigation—in the context of climate change, refers to actions that help reduce the rate or severity of climate change by reducing the amount of greenhouse gases being released or by increasing the removal of greenhouse gases from the atmosphere

mutually beneficial—describes a relationship between two organisms (people, other animals, plants) in which both benefit

mycelium—the vegetative (non-reproducing) part of a fungus, made up of a mass of delicate threads (called hyphae) that spread through the soil or other habitat and absorb the nutrients the fungus needs

mycorrhizal fungi—fungi which form a mutually beneficial relationship with plants or trees

nonviolent direct action—actions that confront, disrupt and actively oppose, without using violence, something that is believed to be harmful or unjust. For example, boycotts, strikes, sit-ins or road blockades

nurse log—a dead tree that has fallen over and lies on its side in a forest, and as it decomposes provides moisture, nutrients and habitat to many plants and animals

nutrients—sources of nourishment, such as minerals and food, that are required by plants and animals for growth and survival

old-growth forest—forests that are dominated by old trees and have certain ecological and structural characteristics that come with age, such as the presence of younger trees among the old ones, dead standing snags and lots of fallen logs

omnivore—an animal that feeds on both plants and other animals

organic food—food that is grown without the use of chemical pesticides or fertilizers

organism—a living being, such as a plant, animal, insect, bacteria or fungus

potlatch—a sacred cultural feast with dancing and gifts, held by First Nations to mark major events like births, deaths, the transfer of names and other important community business

precautionary principle—a guideline that advises us to avoid actions or policies that *might* cause harm to the public or to the environment, even if the risks are not fully known

predator—an animal that lives by capturing and eating other animals

prey—an animal that is hunted and eaten by other animals

residential schools—boarding schools for First Nations children who were forcibly taken from their families; run by churches in partnership with the federal government

second-growth forest—a forest that grows back after a major disruption, such as clear-cut logging or a fire

sit-in—an organized protest in which a group of people seat themselves inside a business or in a public place to draw attention to an issue or shut down a harmful activity; protesters refuse to leave until their concerns are addressed or they are arrested or evicted by force

snag—a dead tree that is still standing

species—a group of closely related organisms that share similar characteristics and are capable of producing offspring. Western red cedars,

grizzly bears, bald eagles and humans are some examples of species

streamkeepers—people of all ages who are helping to protect, restore and monitor salmon habitat

sustainable—capable of being maintained at a steady level within the limits of what an ecosystem can support without exhausting natural resources or causing ecological damage

tar sands—an area of industrial development in northern Alberta, where boreal forests are being removed in order to mine a tar-like fossil fuel called bitumen, which can be turned into oil through a water- and energy-intensive process that contaminates water and releases greenhouse gases

tide pool—a small pool of seawater along rocky areas of the ocean shoreline that remains full of water even after the tide has gone out and provides important habitat for intertidal plants and animals

topsoil—the top layer of soil, containing many microorganisms and the nutrients that plants need

water cycle—also called hydrological cycle; the continuous process by which water evaporates from plants, ground surfaces and bodies of water, rises into the atmosphere, forms clouds and is returned back to earth in the form of rain and snow

Resources

Please go to **www.greatbearrainforest.ca**
for a complete list of resources.

Further Reading

George, Chief Earl Maquinna. *Living on the Edge: Nuu-Chah-Nulth History from an Ahousaht Chief's Perspective*. Winlaw: Sono Nis Press, 2003.

Glavin, Terry. *The Last Great Sea: A Voyage through the Human and Natural History of the North Pacific Ocean*. Vancouver: Greystone Books (co-published by The David Suzuki Foundation), 2000.

Hill, Julia Butterfly. *The Legacy of Luna: The Story of a Tree, a Woman and the Struggle to Save the Redwoods*. New York: HarperOne, 2001.

Hoose, Phillip. *It's Our World, Too! Stories of Young People Who Are Making a Difference*. New York: Farrar, Straus and Giroux, 2002.

Kelsey, Elin. *Not Your Typical Book About the Environment*. Toronto: Owlkids, 2010.

King, Thomas. *The Truth About Stories*. Toronto: Anansi, 2003.

Leonard, Annie. "The Story of Stuff." The Story of Stuff Project video, accessed March 2011. www.storyofstuff.com.

McAllister, Ian. *The Last Wild Wolves: Ghosts of the Rainforest*. Vancouver: Greystone Books, 2007.

McAllister, Ian, Karen McAllister and Cameron Young. *The Great Bear Rainforest: Canada's Forgotten Coast*. Madeira Park: Harbour Publishing, 1997.

McAllister, Ian, and Nicholas Read. *The Salmon Bears: Giants of the Great Bear Rainforest*. Victoria: Orca Book Publishers, 2010.

McAllister, Ian, and Nicholas Read. *The Sea Wolves: Living Wild in the Great Bear Rainforest*. Victoria: Orca Book Publishers, 2010.

Raven Tales. Animated Aboriginal Folklore, acccessed June 2011. www.raventales.com.

Index

Page numbers in **bold** refer to images.

Acknowledgments

Living at the edge between land and sea has shaped me and shaped this book. I give thanks to my parents, Maggie and Phil, for putting me in kayaks and hiking boots at a young age, opening my eyes to the wonders and the struggles of the world, and believing in me.

Thank you to everyone who has welcomed me into their communities in the Great Bear Rainforest. To those of you who have shared your stories in this book, my deepest gratitude. I am humbled by the strength and generosity and spirit of all who work to sustain the cultures and protect the ecosystems of this coast. It is an honor to know and work with you.

Thank you to the many people who supported and encouraged me throughout the long process of writing this book. Your patience has been remarkable, and much appreciated. Thank you to everyone at Orca Book Publishers for offering me this opportunity and putting so much effort behind my words. Special thanks to my editor, Sarah Harvey, for her gentle guidance and hard questions, and to Teresa Bubela and Nadja Penaluna for making the book look amazing. Thank you to my colleagues at Sierra Club BC: you inspire, you cheer me on, and I am so grateful for all the support. A big thank-you to everyone who reviewed all or parts of the book, answered questions and provided feedback: Maggie Ziegler, Phil Vernon, Erin Griffiths, Colin Campbell, Lisa Matthaus, Jens Wieting, Audrey Roburn, Andy MacKinnon, Ian McAllister and Sonora Godfrey. Special thanks to Jess Housty and Lynne Hill. Any factual errors are my own.

Beyond words, images show how special the Great Bear Rainforest truly is. Thank you to all of the photographers who have so generously provided such stunning and beautiful photos. Special thanks to Douglas Neasloss (dougneasloss.com), Marven Robinson, Andrew S. Wright (cold-coast.com), Thomas P. Peschak (www.thomaspeschak.com), Cristina Mittermeier (cristinamittermeier.com), TJ Watt (utopiaphoto.ca), Mike Ambach (mikeambach.com), Jens Wieting, Ian McAllister, Jared Hobbs (hobbsphotos.com), Qqs (Eyes) Projects Society, Greenpeace, Save Our Seas Foundation, and the International League of Conservation Photographers. Thanks also to Robert D. Turner, Sarah Turner, Daniel Beltra, Chip Vinai, Miles Ritter, Marshall Maher, Mark Worthing, Kate Brauer, Morgan Hocking, Scott Rehmus, ZoAnn Morten, Wayne Worden, Paul Nicklen, Brian Van Wyk, Kiku Dhanwant, the Haida Gwaii Local Foods Processing Co-op, Sierra Youth Coalition, Frances Litman and the family of Nonnie Florence Davidson. Thank you to Dave Leversee for making the maps, and to everyone who helped me find photos, especially Nori Sinclair, Aube Giroux, Jess Housty and Lynne Hill.

Finally, my appreciation and gratitude to everyone out there who is working to make this world a better place to live; you know who you are. You inspire me and give me hope for the future. Together we stand tall.